PREHISTORIC BURIALS OF KASHMIR

PREHISTORIC BURIALS OF KASHMIR

A.K. SHARMA

AGAM KALA PRAKASHAN
DELHI

First Published : 1998

ISBN : 81-7320-036-X

Published By :
Dr. Agam Prasad, M. A. Ph. D. Diploma in Museology
for AGAM KALA PRAKASHAN
34, Central Market, Ashok Vihar,
Delhi-110052,
Ph. : 7212195, 7401485-6-7
Fax : 91-11-7401485

Composed By :
Printo Art Services
2527-A, Tri Nagar,
Delhi-110035
Ph.: 7197519

Printed at : Goyal Offset Printers Delhi-35

Printed in INDIA

To

The Peace Loving

People of Jammu, Kashmir and

Ladakh

PREFACE

In the archaeological excavations remains of flora and fauna, if carefully collected and scientifically studied, throw light on the environmental and climatic conditions of the ages to which the site belongs. Unfortunately in India, human and animal skeletal remains, now-a-days, don not get the importance in the site, that they deserve. Particularly animal bones are collected like the pottery sherds and sent to the pottery yard, where they are washed with hard brushes, before subjecting them to the thorough scrutiny of an archaeo-zoologist. This process results in the loss of many vital clues and evidences. Due to lack of properly trained physical anthropologists, human skeletal remains and burials are not thoroughly studied and recorded in the field in in-situ condition. Field observations and measurements are most vital and supplementary to laboratory analysis as due to fragile condition of the remains many clues are lost while lifting the bones part by part. It is with the aim of emphasising the importance of careful exposure of the burials and field recordings on them, that this book is being brought out. I hope the details given in the book would be helpful to the excavators and students of field archaeology. To give a comprehensive picture of Burzahom burials field observations and laboratory observations have been combined.

During my field work at Burzahom, Shri T.N. Khazanchi, the excavator of the site provided me all the facilities required for which I am grateful to him. In the site my colleagues S/Shri S.L. Sali, B.M. Pande, R.K. Pant and S.S. Saar extended all the help I needed for the execution of my work. I am thankful to them all. Late Shri V. Dutta and Shri Puran Singh very ably captured the operations and photographed the burials from all possible angles, with movie and still cameras, respectively. It is because of their untiring efforts that the photographic evidences are with us. I am grateful to them. Models of the skeletons were prepared by S/Shri T.N. Padmanabhan and Sudershanam under very odd circumstances and in biting cold. They deserve all praise for the wonderful Job they did. I am also grateful to all the members of the then Frontier Circle, Srinagar for making our stay at Burzahom memorable one. During my first seasons work at burzahom, my wife Smt. Kusum Sharma was with me to share with me all the inconviniences of field life and vagries of Kashmir weather. Due to her presence I could devote my full attention to my job. I am grateful to her.

I can never forget the sincerity, devotion and simplicity of the Burzahom folks who worked with me in the site and who helped me and my wife in the camp throughout our stay. I still remember the fatherly figure of late Shri Pursottam, the wonderful driver-mechanic who ferried us in most difficult circumstances.

In the completion of this book, Shri B.M. Pande gave me learned suggestions and other help for which I am thankful to him. Illustration are courtesy Archaeological Survery of India and Anthropological Survey of India.

I am also grateful to Shri M.S. Mani my colleague in Archaeological Survey of India and in Indira Gandhi National Centre for the Arts, who helped me in arranging the illustrations. Schematic section of Burzahom is by Shri S.S. Saar. Some of the photographs are by shri B.R. Rajput and line drawings of Gulfkral are by Shri J.S. Dubey, all my colleagues in Archaeological Survey of India. I am indebted to them. I am grateful to Shri Rakesh Khanduri, my colleague in IGNCA who helped me in preparing the index.

I hope this little humble effort on my part will fill up some of the gap in the Prehistory of Kashmir.

A.K. SHARMA

LIST OF ILLUSTRATIONS

CONTENTS

1

INTRODUCTION

Jammu, Kashmir and Laddhakh are ancient lands where man lived right from the Palaeolithic limes onwards. Evidences regarding palaeolithic culture are so far scantly due to lack of research in this direction but from neolithic onwards the area abounds in sites and monuments. During historical times the king of Kashmir extended his domain even upto Gujrat. The valley was a great centre of learning. The origin of Kashmir Neolithic was somewhere in Central Asia. It started, in the valley, before C. 2920 B.C. and continued upto C. 1700 B.C. around which time a new wave of people entered the valley with the knowledge of Megalithic building, rice and iron. An interesting feature of the Kashmir valley Neolithic is its burials, both human and animal alongwith the human beings their pet animals such as dogs were also buried.

Researchers like Southworth [1 & 2] have found some indication that there might even have been some ancestral Sino-Tibetan language (s) in the region, which would correlate with the archaeological materials from Kashmir as found at Burzahom and Gufkral. Tikkanen [3] suggests that the ancestral tongue related to modern Burushaski was spoken in Kashmir during the third millennium.

Encouraged by the environments of the enchanting valley, as soon as I got the opportunity to work there, particularly on the unique burial systems, comming to light for the first time, I rushed to the site with my wife. Though it was our first visit to the valley, I found every one, right from my collegues in the Archaeological Survery of India to the local people

---

1. Southworth, Franklin C., Cereals in South Asian prehistory a look at the linguistic evidence. In K.A.R. Kennedy and G.L. possehl, eds;, *Ecological Backgrounds of South Asian Prehistory.* Ithaca; Cornell University South Asia occasional papers and Thesis No. 4:52-74, 1976.
2. Southworth, Franklin C. Linguitics and archaeology; prehistoric implications of some south Asian Plant names; In Gregory L. Possehl, ed. *South Asian Archaeology Studies*, Delhi, 1982.
3. Tikkanen, Bertil, on Burushaski and others, ancient substrata in north western South Asia. *Studia Orientalia*, 1988.

eager to help us. They spoke only Kashmiri and understood few words of Hindi, but language of signs is the easiest medium of expression and understanding. Of course at times, this led to some funny incidents. Once my wife asked Khazar Ganai to bring some potatoes from the village, the word used was 'All'. Khazar Ganai nodded his head as if he has understood fully. Minutes later he appeared with a big 'Kaddu' i.e., Cucumber. All of us laughed and laughed. We had the fortune of enjoying the sparkling red diamonds of 'Anar' every day after lunch as Khazar Canai will keep them ready on a plate. There was no dearth of apples and almonds. Few of our friends coming from Delhi, eager to eat more of the raw almonds, had to pay with *spoiled stomachs*. As the work could not be completed by the end of October, we were forced to stay on till the first week of December, by which time the temperatures had gone appreciably low which were too low particularly for my wife who had never experienced such severe cold. When we ran short of warm clothings it was Khazar Ganai who brought a number of hand woven woolen blankets from his house and saw that we are comfortable. My friend Shri Jassu Ram Batra, who was also drafted from our Delhi office to take care of drawings of Burzahom excavations was kind enough to get quilts prepared for us at Delhi and bring them to Burzahom. Due to lack of knowledge and experience we did not use fur boots when it became too cold. The result was disastrous for my wife, whoe feet got swollen and started giving unbearable pain. After we had shifted to the guest house at Srinagar, it wa the local chowkidar there who came out with indigenous way of treatment. Seeing the painful condition of my wife, the elderly father figure, prepared hot water and dipped slices of 'Salzam' in it. He treated the feet of my wife by rubbing 'Salzam' slices on them. The results were instantaneously wonderful. Within two days swelling and pain disappeared.

It was sometime during November, 1962, we were caught amidst the Chinese attack over India. 'Chusul' the highest airport in the world, was the target of Chinese. Almost throughout the day Indian Air-Force planes used to make sorties with supplies to 'Chusul' right over our tents. On 13th November, 1962 as it suddenly started snowing heavily and as the roads to Srinagar were going to be blocked, almost all the officials returned back to Srinagar. In the camp myself, my wife, Shri Padmanabhan, the wonderful modeller, and Shri R.K. Pant, were left with essential supplies almost exhausting. On the night of 14th Nov. 1962, due to heavy snow fall our tent fell-down, in the mid-night. Myself and my wife immediately shifted ourselves from the top of our bed to the underneath of the 'charpoy' as the roof of tent rested over the 'Charpoy'. Again it was the local people who came to our rescue and kept us supplying with rice, potatoes and eggs as these were the only things available with them. It was at this point that my wife, a strict vegetarian, had to resort to eating eggs.

Even during these very cold days in our young enthusiasm and eagerness to produce something outstanding myself and shri Padmanabhan continued to work over the burials. I, writing detailed field notes and treating the bones with chemicals and Shri Padmanabhan preparing the life size models of human skeletons using rubber mould technique. As the weather was too harsh, almost always raining or snowing we had to work inside the deep trenches by covering them with corrugated tin sheets and holding the superb warming 'Kangadis' to warm our fingers. It was these 'Kangadis' that actually saved us from severe cold as we, after few days of inconveniences, became adept to sleep with them, holding them between of our palms inside the quilts. After few days of snowing, when all the hills were fully covered with snow, there was bright sun-shine. As there was snow everywhere in the camp myself and my wife, fow whom this was the first snowy experience of life, enjoyed every bit of it. With awe in our eyes we watched sparrows eating snow. My friend Shri Puran Singh Jamwal, the artful photographer and stage artist photographed us eating snow, playing in snow and of course me in borrowed coat and tie from shri B.M. Pande. All the burials were well recorded on the drawing sheets by Shri Sadhu Singh Saar, fully photographed by Shri Puran Singh and models were prepared in 1962 by Shri T.N. Padmanabhan and in 1963 by Shri Sudershanam. As per original plans a museum was to come up at the site where antiquities, models and photgraphs were to be displayed. so fat nothing has happened though burzahom excavation opened a new chapter in the prehistory of the Indian subcontinent. On my part the detailed field notes on human and animal burials were written in 1962 and 1963 and immediately submitted to the excavator of the site. It is distressing, particularly for me, to find that they had not seen the light of the day even after more than thirty years. In the morphological report of the human skeletal remains published by the Anthropological Survey of India in 1980 with the title 'Human Remains from Burzahom', though it is stated on page 2 'A field note on the mode of burials presented by A.K. Sharma is appened at the end (see Appendix)', the same has not been appended as there is no appendix in the book. At what stage it was suddenly decided to black out the appendix, it is difficult for me to say. After waiting for long years for Burzahom excavations report to be completed, I decided to bring the field notes alongwith the articles published by me on Burzahom human and animal burials, to the notice of the scholars and students, in the form of the present book, lest people may say Sharma did not write and submit the field notes.

In 1981 and 1982 I got the chance to excavate another important neolithic site of Gufkral in Kashmir valley. (Pl.II) As the funds put at my disposal were limited, I decided to take vertical trenches almost in the centre of the mound. The results were more encouraging then at Burzahom. Here at Gufkral, for the first time in the neolithic context of India, we met with the basal Aceramic neolithic levels datable to the beginning of the third millennium B.C. (after MASCA correction). As the vertical dig was limited to only 4.25x4.25 m. single row of trenches, the advantages of area excavations were lacking. The dig did reveal the nature of habitational patterns of different phases and periods of occupation and good number of antiquities but did not yield any burials. It is likely that in the limited dig we did not strike at the spots were burials were located. But I noticed doing surface explorations, a number of circular human burials concentrated on the north-eastern corner of the mound. It was decided to tackle these burials in the third season i.e., in 1983 but due to some reasons Dr. K.D. Banergee, who was my boss then in the Prehistory Branch of Archaeological Survey of India, did not allow me to continue the work at Gufkral in the third season. As I was suddenly shifted to Calcutta, the process of writing the report was stopped. After every seasons dig I produced the results in the form of articles which were immediately published in various research journals and books. This I did with the intention of bringing the results of our excavation and reasearches to the notice of scholars without any loss of time, so that they may not loose their importance. I still long to write and publish the full report of the excavations at Gufkral for the reasons a) Gufkral being the most important Neolithic site of the north, and b) there is hardly any possibility of Burzahom report seeing the light of the day.

In this book I had incorporated the gist of my articles on human and animal burials from Burzahom published elsewhere and notes from the report on 'Human remains from Burzahom' by S/Shri Arabinda Basu and Anandi Pal of Anthropological Survey of India. I am grateful to them. I do hope this book will atleast fill up a very small portion of the gap that exists in the neolithic scence of Kashmir valley due to non publication of Burzahom and Gufkral excavation reports. As could be seen by comparing the measurements on various parts of the skeletal remains taken in the field in in situ condition and in the laboratory, the field measurements play important roel, if taken accuarately, in arriving at the conclusions determining the morphological features of the people who inhabited the valley during neolithic and megalithic times for nearly 2000 years without any break. The results clearly show that the neolithic and megalithic people of Kashmir were the ancestors of present day long headed and tall Kashmiris. They also exhibit very close racial affinity with the pepple of Harappa R. 37, morphological reuslts of which are known and as per fiedl observations with the harappnas of kalibangan and interestingly with the tall and long headed people who occupy the plains of Jammu, Panjab and Haryana today. These affinities also clearly point out that though the people of a particular region may originate from a common source, one section way remain confined to the same culture and way of life for thousands of years depending on the geographical and ecologica environments of the area of occupation where as the other group may advance further and achieve higher goals of civilization as happened in case of neolithic people of Kashmir and Harappans of the Plains respectively.

Everyone thought and thinks that such a beautiful and fertile valley was occupied by the people who appeared from across the borders, some time during the neolithic times. This may be true but only partly as, the discovery of Early Stone Age tools at Pahalgam and elsewhere in Jammu and Kashmir, clearly show that 'Man' right from the begining of pleistocene times lived in the area and slowly evolved. The harsh climatic condition, as per evidences throughout the world, now pouring in, never deterred the Homo Sapiens Sapiens from occupying both heavily snow covered and terribly hot mountains and deserts. Evidences from Gufkral and Burzahom indicate that during Neolithic and Megalithic times new waves of people did come hom across the borders and got themselves assimilated with the less advanced locals who readily accepted their advanced and beneficial ways of living and technologies.

So far as the animal burials at Burzahom are concerned, it was for the first time in the Indian sub-continent, particularly in the neolithic context that so many systematic burials of animals, both animals buried separately and animals buried with human beings, were encountered, exposed and studied. Dog, Wolf and Himalayan Ibex were the three animals who found a systematic burial at Burzahom is amazing. As per the evidences, the same type of circular pits, plastered with 'Chunam' from inside were used for animals also as were used for neolithic people of Burzahom. Both were buried inside the habitation area, below the floor of the house. In both the cases the body was kept in north-south orientation, with the skull towards north, facing east or west. The parts of the pet animals like dog which were buried alongwith the human body were also invariably treated with red-ochre solution like the human skeletal parts. Obviously this treatment was effected when after the decompostion of the flesh the bones were re-exposed. In some cases in the same grave pit more than one animals were interned. putting them at different levels of the deep pit. Neolithic people of Burzahom though great hunters; the direct depicting hunting scene. where tow neolithic folks have been shown aiming their arrows towards a stag from front and back, when the sun was shining bright over the horizon; were also great artistes. Archaeologists generally believe that early man was mostly dependent on hunting of animals for their food requirements, but this is not true. He was as good in food gathering as in hunting, as evidenced by the type of bone and stone tools found in excavations. This becomes more clear if we study the living primitive tribes living under similar environmental conditions and almost at the same stage of civilization even to-day.

2

GEOLOGY AND ENVIRONMENT

Kashmir contains, within a small geographical area, one of the first developments of the stratified record in the Indian sub-continent. A very large section of the fossiliferous geological record is exhibited in the hills and mountains surrounding the beautiful valley of Kashmir (Pl.I). The 'bone bed' at Sombur. 19 kms south-east of Srinagar, available in the exposed section of Jhelum gives a unique insight into the nature of the overlying beds where Triassic rock is overlain by Pleistocene beds. In the light-grey to yellowish clay fresh water-shells, fish vertebrae and bones, lacerated plant fragments (Equisetum like forms), broken limb bones of artiodactyla mammals and elephant remains occur. The fish bones form clusters, although vertebrae are found singly throughout the clay. The curious mixture of shells with bones of mammals, fish and birds, in a thin clay bed, signifies shore deposit of a lake. The absence of silt and sand and the abundance of delicate fish vertebrae and isolated mammal remains and teeth indicate deposition in quiet water. Offshore currents and wave action were presumably sufficiently powerful to lacerate the stranded and bogged bodies of land and water animals which were probably preyed on by large birds. Hora who studied the fossil fish remains is of the opinion that they belong to the Schizothoracine, now living in Kashmir as lake or sluggish water forms. The bone bed represents the first interglacial shore deposit.

The conglomerate above the bone bed shows well-assorted constituents such as lime-stone, trap and quartzite with a few subangular boulders. The pebbles are worn to a degree as might be expected from components washed out of a delta or fan. This might have been the origin of the conglomerate, far it reappears along the mountain side near krew, some 6.5 kms. northeast of Sombur.

Physical Features

There is a close uniformity in physical features and geological constitution of the sub-Himalayan tract from Rawalpindi to Dehradun covered by the Siwalik and Sirmur rock systems. The Central Himalayan axis, after its bifurcation near Kulu, runs as one the high twin peaks of Nunkum (23,444'); the other branch runs due west as the high range of Pir Panjal. Between these two branches of the crystalline axis of the Himalayas lies a longitudinal valley with a south-east to north-west trend, some 135 kms. long and 40 kms broad in its middle. The total area of Kashmir valley is 3040 sq. km. The mean height above the sea is nearly 1730 m. The mountain ranges which surround it all round except the narrow gorge of the Jhelum at Baramula, attain to the north-east and north-west, a high general altitude, some peaks rising above 6000m. On the south-western border the Pir Panjal is of comparatively lower altitude having mean elevation of 4660 m. The outermost ranges of the Kashmir Himalya rise from the plains of the Punjab, commencing with a gentle slope from Jammu attain to about 670 m. altitude, and then end abruptly in steep, almost perpendicular escarpments inwards. The longitudinal or strike valleys (the basins of subsequent streams) inside the hills are of more frequent occurrence in the eastern parts of the Himalayas, being known there as 'duns'. In the Jammu hills the extensive duns of Udhampur and Kotli are quite typical. The Kashmir valley itself may be taken as an exaggerated instance of dun in the middle Himalaya. These outer hills formed entirely of the younger tertiary rocks rarely attain to greater altitude than 1350 m. Ranges situated more inwards, and formed of older Tertiary rocks reach the higher altitude, of about 2000 to 2670 m.

Pir Panjal range was uplifted to 5000 m. during the Pleistocene period. To-day it grows paperbirch, rhododendron and juniper. The rolling upland is covered by alpine type meadows termed *maar* in the local dialect.

Karewas (Pl. II)

Pleistocene or post-Pliocene deposits of the nature of fluviatile, lacustrine or glacial, have spread over many parts of Kashmir and occupy a wide superficial extent. Of these the most interesting as well as conspicuous examples are the fresh water (fluviatile and lacustrine) deposits, found as low flat mounds, bordering the slopes of the mountains above the modern alluvium of the Jhelum. These are known as *Karewas* in Kashmiri. The *Karewa* formation occupies nearly half the area of the valley; it had a width of from 12.5 to 25 km. alongwith its south-West side and extends for a length of nearly 80 kms from Shopphiyan to Baramulla. The *karewas* are mostly horizontally stratified deposits consisting of beds of fine-grained sand, loam, blue sandy clays with lenticular bands of gravelly conglomerate. At some localities the finer sands and clays show laminations of the nature of "varving" - alternating laminae of different colour and grain indicating periods of summer melting of ice and of winter freezing. Evidence of oscillation of the glacial climate is recorded in the *Karewa* deposits. At the end of the ice-age there was a forest period in the Kashmir valley. *Karewa* has been traced continuously upto almost the summit of the Pir Panjal.

According to some observers this part of the Himalayas underwent for distinct glaciations, separated by interglacial warm periods. Indication of these successive glaciations are present in the glacier moraines and drifts which fill the ice-eroded, characteristically shaped tributary valleys and in the system of river-terraces in the upper reaches of the main valley of Jhelum, into which the moraine deposits gradually merge. The moraines of the Pleistocene glaciation are well preserved on the Sind and Liddar valleys. Moraines belonging to three or four successive glacial advances, inter-bedded with the *Karewa* deposits at various levels, have been recognised by De Terra. The terminal moraines of the latest glacial period are seen capping the top beds of the upper *Karewas*. De Terra and Paterson discovered five terraces in the Kashmir valley. Terraces I and III were caused by erosion during interglacial periods when the ice melted and great streams of water were released. Terraces II, IV and V were aggradational and were formed due to the filling up of the valley by ice. The only radio-carbon dated pollen sequence from the bogs of Toshmaidan in Kashmir shows that deglaciation here started around 15,000 B.P. The pollen profiles yielded a cold-warm-cold sequence starting from the date of deglaciation.

The Neolithic settlers occupied the commending terraces of the Karewas. At Haigam, the pollen profile shows clearance of pine forest which may have something to do with agriculture activity.

3
THE SITES

B*urzahom :* (34° 10'; 73°54'), district Srinagar is located 16Km north -east of Srinagar, about 1800m. above sea level. The Megalithic menhirs here situated on a Karewa mound were first noticed by de Terra and Paterson, in 1939, who collected some bone and stone tools in a short excavataion. Extensive excavation were conducted on behalf of Archaeological survery of India under the direction of shri T.N. Khazanchi from 1960 to 1971, which brought to light a fourfold sequence of cultures; Periods I and II, Neolithic; Period III Megalithic; and Period IV, early historical.

Period I has revealed dwelling pits, circular or oval and pit chambers, square to rectangular in shape. The pottery of this period is mostly crude and handmade, the colour being chiefly steel-grey and shades of dull-red, brown and buff. Mat impression on the flat base of pots were noticed. The artefacts include well polished bone and stone tools. The main type in bone are harpoons, needles with or without eyes, awls, spear-points, arrow heads, daggers and scrapers. Stone tools include axes, chisels, adzer, pounders, mace-heads, points and picks. No burials, human or animal were encountered from this period.

In period II semi-subterranean pits and pit chambes were filled up and plastered with mud and sometimes covered with a thin coal of red ochre. The super structure was built of timber, wattle and daub 'having thatched roofs.

Human and animal burials were found of which human burials were both primary and secondary in oval pits, mostly dug in the floor of the house and filled with ash, stone pieces and pot sherds. Alongwith the human burials, bones of dog and deer were also buried in oval pits inside the houses. Apart from bone and stone objects recovered similar to perioded I, harvestors in stone objects recovered similar to period I, harvestors in stone and bone - rectangular or semicircular in form with a sharp cutting edge and pierced holes at the upper end, double edged picks in stone and long needles with or without eye in love were also recovered. A single copper arrowhead is also reported form the last phase of this period. Pottery is generally hand made with burnished black ware of medium fabric making its appearance. The most important find was a wheel made red ware with 950 cornelian and agate beads.

Period III ushered the era arrival of megalithic people at the site who erected members in honour of their dead ones.

In order to have a correct picture of neolithic and megalithic chronology of Kashmir Valley the Culture sequence of - Gufkral are being described here in some detail :

Gufkral (literally *Guf*-cave, *Kral*-potter), a site inhabited by potters who are utilizing the caves cut into the Karewa, was excavated by the Prehistory Branch of Archaeological Survey of India in 1981 and 1982. On the slopes of the 35m. high mound, there are a number of caves, both single and multichambered with pillars. Some, particularly on the south-eastern side are being occupied by *Krals* both for residential and storage purposes. Others, which are deserted, had their openings closed due to collapse of the earth. Enquiries made so far have revealed that the oldest *Kral*, a centenarian, was born in one of these caves.

The site, Lat. 35°54' N, Long 75°60' E, is situated 41Km. south-east of Srinagar near Tahsil town of Tral in District Pulwama of Jammu and Kashmir State. It can be approached by Awantipur-Dodsar-Tral road. It is located on an extensive deposit of upper *Karewa* adjacent to village Ban-Mir in between two nallahs that join Jhelum nearly 10Km. to the west. At the top the mound measures 400m. long north-south and 75m. wide east-west. Maximum height of the mound from the road level on the Western side is 35m. On the northern extension of the mound in the exposures a thick deposit of conglomerate could be seen by cross bedded sand, light yellow slit and Karewa. The conglomerate is composed of lime stone, trap and quartzite with boulders.

On the eastern edge of the mound, almost in the centre, are found a number of menhirs on the slope. None of them, however, is in its original and upright position. Few have rolled down to the bottom of the mound and are being used for washing clothes by the *Krals*. (Pl. IV)

2. CULTURE SEQUENCE

The site was explored in 1962-63 by the then Frontier Circle of Archaeological Survey of India. The dig was restricted to almost the centre of the mound, where a maximum of 3.10m. of habitational deposit was encountered over the natural soil. On the northern side of the mound, 5m. of deposit is expected as indicated by rain gullies and side scrapings. Some scrapings were also made in rain gullies which revealed oval and rectangular pits.

The excavation revealed five periods of occupation :- (Fig. 3)

Period IA - Aceramic Neolithic

Period IB - Early Neolithic

Period IC - Late Neolithic

Period II - Megalithic

Period III - Historical

Each period of occupation was clearly sealed by a floor of the subsequent period.

The most significant finds of this excavation were: (a) Presence of a well-defined Aceramic Neolithic level, the deposit varying from 35cm. to 1.10m. (b) Identification of cereal grains and (c) Faunal assemblage dominated by wild animals in the lower levels slowly leading almost exclusively to domesticated ones in the middle and upper levels of Neolithic period.

3. PERIODWISE DESCRIPTION

A. PERIOD IA. ACERAMIC NEOLITHIC PERIOD

The Aceramic Neolithic Period having a deposit of 35m. to 1.10 m. was sealed by a continuous floor of yellow compact clay mixed with 'Chunam' running in all the trenches. Two phases of occupation could be distinctly marked by the presence of two floor levels, one on the top of the natural soil and the other after a deposit of nearly 30-35cm.

(i) Settlement Pattern

Settlement pattern consisted of large and small dwelling pits cut into loessic deposits, being circular or oval on plan with narrow mouths and wide bottoms. They varied in diameter from 3.80m. to 1.50m. at the top. Large dwelling pits generally belonged to phase 1 and were only 20 to 30cm. deep unlike dwelling pits at Burzahom which were very deep (upto 3.96m.). These pits were surrounded by storage pits and hearths. A number of post-holes were noticed around the pits and the hearths to support the super structure of grass and reed. Recovery of mud chunks with reed impressions indicates that most probably the bases of the super structures were plastered with mud to give strength and prevent entry of water and snow from sides. In phase 1, the floors of the dwelling pits and storage pits, all cut into the loessic deposit (top of natural soil) and their working levels in a wide area, were plastered with red ochre paste. No such treatment was available in the floors belonging to phase 2. Some dwelling pits cut in phase 1 were subsequently enlarged and used in phase 2 also as indicated by the successive deposits inside these pits. In phase 2, two chambered dwelling pits were also available and were deeper then their counterparts in phase 1.

Hearths of phase 1 were rectangular in shape whereas in phase 2, both circular and rectangular hearths made of burnt clay were available. One of the circular hearths had its floor and sides plastered with mud. This circular hearth was 93cm. in diameter (outer) and 30cm. deep. It had post-holes on its outer periphery. The presence of these post-holes and large quantity of ash from inside the hearth along with pebbles, indicates that the animals hunted were roasted by hanging over the fire in the hearth supported by the poles.

The maintenance of floors, covering a wide area around pits, shows that people used to live outside during warm seasons and occupy dwelling pits in winter, but roasting of food (both flesh, tubers and grains) was done only outside as no hearths or fire place were found inside the dwelling pits.

(ii) Artifacts

Among the artifacts used by the settlers are polished stone celts, both finished and unfinished, stone point, with one and both ends sharp, made out of Himalayan cist, one broken unfinished ring stone, pounders and querns. A large quern with a depression on the working surface and showing red ochre paste adhered to it was recovered from the red ochre treated floor near the dwelling pit in one of the trenches.

Bone tools, both polished throughout the body and only at the working tips were recovered. They were shaped out of long bones, splinters and horns. Most of these were points and arrow-heads. besides, awls, some pierces and scrapers were also recovered. Of special mention however, is a polished bone needle with damaged eye. In majority of the tools, tips have been charred to give the required strength to the working ends. Piercers were used for making incision and tearing open the flesh after the animal was killed and skin removed, whereas scrapers were used to scrap out fat from flesh. Bone tools were mostly made from the green bones, bones of sheep, goat, cervus and ibex being generally preferred. Advantage was taken of the natural curves, depressions and articulation ends of various parts for making different types of tools. Arrowheads were tiny in size like microliths with only their tips charred and polished. Among the ornaments recovered were one cylindrical highly polished spacer bone bead and two steatite beads, one cylindrical and another barrel shaped. Peace of a terracotta marble was also recovered.

(iii) Animal Remains (Fig. 4)

The animal remains amply demonstrate that in the Aceramic Neolithic period at Gufkral people were predominantly dependant on wild game. Domestication of a selected variety was just being introduced. The animals represented were wild sheep *(Ovis orientalis)*, wild goat *(Capra aegagrus)* wild cattle *(Bos namadicus)*, Red deer *(Cervus elephus)* wolf *(Canis lupus)*, Himalayan Ibex *(Capra Ibex)* and beer *(Ursus)*. Sheep *(Ovis aries)* and goat *(Capra hircus)* were the only animals being domesticated and formed five and three percent of the total assemblage respectively.

With the exception of *Canis lupus*, all the animals hunted were herbivorous. This is possibly due to the fact that animals were easily available in the surrounding hills and slopes.

Ovis, Capra, Bos and Cervus formed the largest percentage of animals hunted, ovis dominating over all. Specimens indicate that cattle and goat were large well built animals whereas sheep was of smaller size.

(iv) Grains

Evidence of grains obtained by floatation technique indicates that in this period people had already realised the importance of grains for food and were either collecting and/or had started cultivation in a limited area. In Kashmir Valley wheat, barley and lentil had much earlier antiquity than rice which is the staple food of Kashmiris in the Valley to-day and which is grown extensively all over the Valley. Wheat, barley and lentil are at present being cultivated in a very limited area and got fillip only with the arrival of Sikhs from outside in recent times. It will be interesting to investigate as to why and when the earlier grains almost totally disappeared from the Valley and were replaced by rice. What were the circumstances that led to total change in the food habit of the people of the Valley? Was rice introduced with the arrival of a new wave of people? Positive evidence in this direction is available from the excavation as rice was recovered from Period II, which is marked with the arrival of Megaliths at the site and could be safely dated to C. 1400B. C. The following grains were recovered from the Aceramic Period:- (i) *Hordeum Vulgare* Linn - row barley; (ii) *Triticum* sp. - wheat; (iii) *Lens esculenta Moonch* - Lentil, Masur and (iv) *Lithospermum arvense* - a weedy plant.

B. PERIOD IB

Aceramic Neolithic Period IA is followed by Neolithic Period IB, without any break. This period is represented by nearly 40cm. thick deposit and yielded a large quantity of charcoal. Hand made Neolithic pottery made its appearance in this period. Overwhelming percentage was of Grey ware with few sherds of rough dull red ware. The shapes represented were big jars, bowls, basins and one stem piece of dish-on-stand in course dull red ware. The decorations included mat impressed bases, pinched designs on the neck region and reed impressions only on exterior and also both on exterior and interior of the pots. Pottery is mostly incompletely oxidised.

(i) Settlement Pattern

Settlement Pattern of this period is indicated by the presence of a 5 to 7 cm. thick floor made of yellow compact clay mixed with 'Chunam' running throughout in almost all the trenches. At some places this floor was repaired atleast 5 to 6 times. The most important building activity of this period was the construction of mud and rubble wall. A compact mud mixed with 'Chunam' wall-like structure running parallel to each other, 70cm. uniformly wide throughout and having almost same space in between, was also encouratered. Total disappearance of dwelling pits from this period shows that the settlement patterns had completely changed with the introduction of pottery. People had now started construction of mud and rubble walls.

The period was also characterised by extensive burning activity. From one of the trenches huge quantity of charcoal and charred wood pieces were recovered. Either Wooden logs stored at one place got burnt down or there was destruction by fire in one of the residential portions.

The artifacts of the period include stone points, ring stone and bone tools (mostly well polished points, piercer cum scrapers shaped out of splinters and spatula).

(ii) Animal Remains & Grains

The period was marked by sudden spurt in domestication of animals like sheep, goat and cattle. Sheep and goat still dominated the faunal assemblage. Percentage of cattle also increased. A sizable quantity of dog bones have also been recovered. Many of the pieces bore cut marks indicating that hunting was still the main source of food. Other animals present were red deer, ibex and bear.

In this period wheat *(Triticum sp.)* barley *(Hordeum Vulgare Linn.)*, Lentil *(Lens esculenta, Moonch)* were the cereal grains represented.

C. Period IC

The Mature phase of Neolithic period is represented by 70 to 75 cm. thick habitational deposit. Pottery consisted of grey ware, burnished grey ware, rough, thick dull red-ware, alongwith black burnished were and wheel turned black burnshed ware; Few examples of red gritty ware are also found. All the shapes of period IB continued. Decoration include mat and cord impressed bases reed and straw impressions to create roughened surface, pinchded designs and incised oblique designs on the neck region. Few sherds with graffitti marks have also been recovered.

(i) Settlement Pattern

The period experienced substantial constructional activity. Three types of structures have come to light-a) a number of circular dwelling pits and storage pits (Silos) were cut through the thick rammed earth. Natural soil was utilised for making the surface hard. Inside the dwelling pits, storage pits and hearth were found. Both, storage and dwelling pits, are quite deep; b) circular huts with mud walls; the thickness of the walls varied from 30to 40 cm; huts having mud and rubble walls. A number of post-holes sorrounded the structure. The pits were probably covered with removable conical thatched roofs made of read and thin branches of willow trees where post-holes were not found around the dwelling and storage pits.

(ii) Artifacts

The period has yielded two polished stone celts, querns, pounders, pestles, ring-stones and sharpners. Stone points which become scarce in period IB, made their appearance again in large numbers. Appearance of double-holed harvesters point out to intense cultivational activities where as spindle whorls of stone and pottery indicate production of thick woolen garments. Other cultural assemblages include terracotta bangles, carnelian beads, cowrie shells and pot-sherds with grafitti marks. Of special significane is the recovery of copper objects, particularly a hair pin with flattened coiled head similar to one found at Chanhudaro, poining to contacts with more advanced cultures of the southern plains.

The period yielded the largest number of bone tools, most of which were well polished points, majority shaped out of splinters. Tips were generally charred and sharp particularly in case of micro-tools like arrow-heads. Few awls, one spatula and harpoons both of bone and stone were other objects recovered.

(iii) Animal remains and gains

By this time the domestication of animals was fully achieved. The entire herd of sheep *(Ovis aries)*, goat *(Copra hircus)* and cattle *(Bos indicus)*. were domsticated. There was considerable reducation in the size of goat and cattle. Sheep and goat continued to dominate the percentage of animals. Percentage of dog increased, Two important new species namely pig *(sus scrofa)* and fish made their appearance. Bones of hare *(Lepus)*, hedge-hog, rodents and beaver were also recovered.

All the grains found in period IB were also recovered from this period.

Complete domestication of animals, and advent of harvesters and spindle whorls indicate that by this lime the neolithic people had adopted a well settled way of life where practicing of agriculture, cattle breeding and herding and weaving of woolen cloth.... .

became the way of life. Hunting was now restricted to red deer and ibex and that too on a limited scale as the percentage of these animals had become considerably reduced in the assemblage. Contacts with the outside world had also started.

D. PERIOD II

Period II which is associated with the arrival of Menhirs on the site has been designated as the Megalithic period. It is represented by nearly 50-60cm. thick habitational deposit. In one of the quadrants near a fallen Manhir, a pit cut in layer 3 containing large quantity of packing material comprising broken pebbles, was exposed. Since not a single menhir is standing and as a huge quantity of broken pebbles are littered all over the site, mostly concentrated near the Manhirs, it appears that the menhirs did not have very deep foundation pits. It also indicates that arrival of menhirs was a much later affair.

The period was marked by the presence of nearly 10cm. thick floor, running throughout, with few breaks due to pit activities. The period also witnessed considerable pit activities. A number of refuge pits sinking right upto the natural soil were cut. From these pits large quantity of pottery and animal bones were recovered.

Burnished Grey ware, gritty red ware and thick dull red ware continued from the previous period but percentage of thick dull red ware and wheel-made pottery increased. Wheel made dull red ware made its appearance. Shapes included jars with shapeless rims, long necked jars, bowls, basins, dish-on-stand and medium sized globular jars. Pinched designs in neck region, incised designs and combed surface obtained by brushing with straw and reeds were available. Vessels with channeled spout were introduced.

Large ring stones, both finished and unfinished were recovered in good number. Stone points had almost disappeared. Other artifacts included a copper point, a wooden bead, pestles, spindle-whorls with medium sized holes and a miniature pot. The only cowrie shell found was from this period. Iron was introduced in this period.

Bone tool industry came to be neglected. Only twenty tools were recovered and that too were not well polished. New innovations were, bone handles shaped mostly from tibia of sheep/goat taking advantage of their shape and bone marrow sockets. They were meant to hold smaller tools for easy operation. A fine cobbler's awl was also recovered.

All the grains of earlier periods continued. Rice (*Oryza sativa* Linn) and millet (*Eleusive coracana*) were introduced in this period.

Animals represented were cattle, sheep, goat, dog, pig, ibex, and fowl. It appears that hunting had almost come to a close for amongst bones of wild animals only those of ibex were recovered. This animal was hunted or captured probably for the sake of horn. Percentage of sheep and goat continued to be higher than that of cattle.

E. PERIOD III

Period III represents the historical occupation on the site. A thick compact floor made of whitish clay was running almost throughout, sealing the Megalithic period. The limited excavation has not yielded any structures except floor levels so far but in the exposed area in other parts of the mound, thick rubble walls could be noticed.

Hand made pottery continued but was dominated by wheel made thin bright red ware. Shapes encountered were jars, bowls, miniature pots, lamps, vases, dishes of Harappan shape, knobbed lids, lid cum bowls, double rimmed pots and cup-on-stand. Few sherds of black painted red ware with stamped designs were also collected. Stone bowls were also found. The artifacts included crude bone tools mostly points, one fine polished bone handle, ring stones, pounders, few stone points and a terracotta huge circular disc (appears to be a hallow on the back of the head of an image).

All the grains of the previous period continued with a definite evidence of rice (*Oryza sativa* Linn) from the lower levels of this period.

Animals bones recovered were identified to be those of cattle, sheep, goat, dog, pig, felis (cat) fowl and rodents.

G. SUMMARY

Excavations at Gufkral have brought to light five period of occupation right from Aceramic Neolithic to Historical Period. It has for the first time firmly established that in the Kashmir Valley also there was an Aceramic Neolithic Period before pottery was introduced. It is in this period that process of domestication of selected species of animals was attempted to. People had also recognised the food value of various grains like wheat and barley and had started collecting them. Bone and stone tools were manufactured. People lived in open and in huts with their bottoms sunk into the loessic deposits in order to protect themselves from gusty freezing winds. They kept the floors tidy and beautiful by painting them with red-ochre. Their main occupation was hunting.

In period IB handmade ceramic was introduced. People had started manufacturing jars, bowls, basins etc. in grey ware and rough dull red ware. There was a change in the settlement pattern. Pits were discarded and mud and rubble walls were constructed. Well polished bone tools were made. There was sudden spurt in the domestication of animals.

By period IC the Neolithic culture had reached the mature stage. In houses, thick whitish floors with 'Chunam' mixed earth were laid. There was now more variety in wares and in their decoration. Large number and variety of well polished bone tools were made. People depended less on larger stone objects. Agriculture was fully established. Weaving of woolen cloth had started. With the domestication of animals and agriculture fully achieved, hunting activities declined. People now got spare time to manufacture ornaments, toys, pots etc.

Period II at Gufkral was marked by the arrival of menhirs. It is yet to be ascertained whether the same people practised the cult of erecting huge memorial stones or a new wave of people had arrived on the site and started living with the original neolithic settlers. With the manhir phase came to the site, wheel made dull red ware, vesseis with channedled spout, iron and copper objects, spindle whorls with medium sized hoes, rice and millet. Bone tool industry was neglected but bone handles were manufactured.

Period III represents the historical phase with wheel made thin bright red ware having jars, bowls, cups-on-stand and lid cum bowls. Stamped designs and black on red paintings were introduced.

The ^{14}C date available for the last stages of Aceramic Neothic levels is 2470+110B.C Hand-made pottery was introduced around 2100 B.C. as the habitational deposit and ^{14}C dates indicate, it took nearly 1000 years for the Aceramic Neolithic settlers to develop the art of pottery making. Contacts with other areas like north China and southern plains were established around the second quarter of second millennium B.C. A fresh wave of people who raised hugemenhirs and brought iron and rice with them. Entered the valley around 1400 B.C. All these calculations are on the basis of uncalibrated dates. The most important point is the date of iron at Gufkral which as per ^{14}C dating comes to around 1400 B.C. thus giving Gufkral another place of pride.

CONTACTS AND COMPARISON

With the discovery of a large number of Neolithic sites, well planned excaations at Burzahom and Gufkaral, and with detailed palaeo-climatic investigations, the enchanting valley has now come to occupy most envying position in the Neolithic map of India. With the ^{14}C dates of various levels available, it is now well established that the neolithic people entered the valley and settle ' doen in the begining of 3rd millennium B.C. and continued to flourish for more than 1500 years till another wave of people with iron and rice entered. The second wave specialised in erecting huge monoliths called menhirs as memorial columns. This was sometime during 1400B.C.. It appears that the new comers did not face any conflict with orininal setters and got assimilated with them. It is yet to be ascertained as to who were they and from where they came to the valley. The evidence available so far clearly shows that the Neolithic people of Kashmir had multi directional contacts. These contacts were of two types, ancestral and trade. While ancestral contacts could be traced to the region of central Asia and west Asia on the basis of cultural equipments, domestication of plants and animals; trade contacts, appear to have been estalished with North China and possibly with the more advanced cultures of the plains south of kashmir valley. Contacts with southern plain are indicated by the presence of certain artifacts like carnelian beads and copper pins. which were imported as well as manufacture techniques borrowed from these areas.

In pottery, bone and stone objects, cereal grain and later on in settlement patterns, the affinities with Saraikhola, Ghaligai, Loebanr III and Bir-Kot-ghundai-IV, of the Swat valley in West Asia.

Recent Discoveries of perforated rectangular harvestors from Loebanr III, similar to those found at Burzahom and Gufkral from the mature Neolithic levels, a 'comma' shapped pendeant of light green jade found both at Gufkral and at loebanr III show very close contacts between Kashmir and Swat during the second quarter of the second millennium B.C. Pit-dwellings and harvesters are the characterstic traits of north Chinese Neolithic culture. Recovery of harvesters and 'comma' shaped pendeant suggests that more than one route connected Northern China with the Northern Valley of Indo-Pakistan sub Continent.

Wheat, einkhorn wheat and barley were domesticated in west Asia by C. 17000 B.C. At Gufkral evidence of wheat, barley, lentil and later on pea right from the aceramic levels also indicate closer contacts with west Asia. While domestication of sheep and goat started during Aceramic period at Gufkral, people mostly depended on wild varieties. This is expected because the Neolithic settlers who entered the valley, though possessed the knowledge of domestication of plants and animals, did not bring with them the domesticated varriety of animals but had to start domesticating process afresh in a new environment, while it was easier to carry with them the doemsticated variety of cereal grains, thought the wild progenitors of domesticates might have been present in the valley. Evidence both at Burzahom and Gufkral on the one hand and at Loebanr and Bir-Kot-Shundai show that around the middle of the second millennium B.C. a change in the settlement pattern occured, when pit-dwellings were abondoned and sealed and over-ground mud and rubble structures were built. This was probably as a result of a significant cultural change which started in the valley around 2000 B.C. (Caliberated). It was by this lime that some new kinds of pottery, including wheel turned and artifacts connected with cultures of the Indus valley, northern India and northen China made their appearance in the valley.

The main evidence for ancestral links comes from the result of study on human skeleal remains from Burzahom. Burzahom crania which are basically long headed resemble the Harappan cemetery R. 37 series more closely. In the Burzahom Neolithic period long headeed dolichocranic individuals were the basic population with features like sloping long and narrow head, protruding occiput, somewhat low receding forehead and medium to prominent supra-orbital ridges. They were of sturdy build with tall to medium statur (common - 1695. 7mm). There is absolutely no evidence of brachycranic skull in either sex. Similar to Nal, Kish-'A', Anau and Hissar III materials, three Burzahom tibia had squatting facet. All these clearly point out that Kashmir Neolithic people belonged to west Asian stock and entered the valley sometime in the begining of third millennium B.C. Total abscence of any mesolithic levels and microliths at Burzahom and Gufkral also indicate that the neolithic culture was an intrusian in the valley.

Evidence from various sites in west Asia clearly suggest that during Mesolithic times in this area a foundation for the settled way of agricultural communities had already been laid 20,000 years ago.

Connecting all the evidence available it appears that the hunter-gatherer communities of central Asia who had managed to adopt to the harsh semi-arid uplands moved to West Asia in the form of pre-neolithic farmers and then developed into first agricultural communities. It was from these stock that a branch entered the Kashmir valley about the beginning of 3rd millennium B.C. in the form of archaic-neolithic settlers.

At Burzahom (Fig. 5) pit dwelling is the most distinctive trait of Period I. Both circular/oval and rectangular/squarish pits were used. Circular pits were bigger and deeper; a large pit had a mouth of 2.7 m diameter expanding to 4.6 m at the base with a depth of about 4 m. One can even see the marks of long celts left during digging. Post-holes around the mouth of these pits must have been used to cover it with a roof thatched with birch and hay whose charred remains have actually been found from such pits. Incidentally, Burzahom in Kashmiri language means the place of birch. Does the name carry the memory of birch thatched roofs all over the place? Alcoves were dug into the walls of the pits; the walls were plastered with mud. In one case, two adjacent pits were connected by an arched corridor. Charcoal, ash, potsheds etc were found from these pits. From some of these pits irregularly dressed conical stones 1 to 1.5 m. long and 20 to 40 cm wide were discovered, though their use is not clear. There were steps cut into the walls to go down into the dwelling pits.

The squarish pits were shallower, compared to the circular ones, with an average depth of 1 m. They had depressions running all around at the bottom of the pit with post-holes at the four corners. They had stone ovens in the centre of such pits, as well as overground. There were refuse pits on the surface. It is therefore obvious that they also lived on the surface whenever the climate was favourable. The number of the squarish pits is larger towards north of the megaliths and of the circular pits on the south. Deeper pits must have been used during winters when the valley becomes snowbound. The shallow pits could have been used during summers.

A variety of ground stone tools were used by these Neolithic people, eg, polished axes, harvesters, pounders, polishers, chisels and maceheads. The harvesters are rectangular stone knives with two or more holes on the blunt side.

The bone tool industry of Burzahom is unique and most developed of all the Neolithic cultures of India. It comprises harpoons, needles, awls, spearpoints, arrowheads, daggers and scrapers.

The Neolithic potters of Burzahom made graceful pots though the use of wheel was not known to them. Pots were made over mats, as is indicated by a variety of weaving patterns impressed on the bottoms of the ports, and were occasionally decorated with incised and notched designs. Colour-range varied from steel-grey to brown.

The earlier dwelling pits were given up in Period II. In fact, they were filled, rammed and sprinkled with red ochre and used as floors for their mud and mud-brick houses. Occasionally, rubble structures are also encountered. Mud platforms, with partitions in them, hearths and oval pits are found inside these houses. Ubiquitous post-holes suggest that thatched roofs were supported by them. In one case 45 post-holes are found arranged, covering an area of five square metres, and probably it could be a community structure. Several successive floors were noticed.

From one of the houses was found a rectangular structure made of upright stones and filled with sand. One of the stones from this structure bore an engraved a hunting scene. Another stone from the same house had a tectiform design.

In stone and bone industries there is a continuity from Period I, though now the tools are better finished and larger in number. A solitary copper arrowhead is reported from the upper levels.

Pottery is still handmade though new shapes and a burnished black ware make their appearance in Period II. Shapes comprise dishes with hollow stand, globular pots, jars, stems with triangular perforation and a funnel shaped vase. In the burnished black were a graceful type is a high-necked jar with a globular body. Towards the close of this period was found a wheelmade red-ware pot containing 950 beads of agate and carnelian. A few painted pots have also been discovered and are likely to be imports. More interesting is a globular pot with a horned deity painted on its shoulders. It has almost an exact parallel in Kot Diji and also in Gumla. This indicates some contact with the Indus and the Baluchi cultures.

No burials were found in Period I, though both inhumation and secondary burials were practiced in Period II. In secondary burials, bones were excarnated by desiccation and treated with red ochre and interred, sometimes in a heap. In the primary burials, except for one solitary example, no red ochre treatment was given. Primary burials of both children and adults were placed in a couched, embryonic position. Skulls were placed either along a north-east or south-east direction. The adult graves were plastered with lime. There were no grave goods, except for the occasional beads which were worn by the dead. The burials are all inside the habitation. At times animal bones, generally of dogs, are also found in the graves which may indicate a practice of burying the pets with their masters. In one skull seven finished and four unfinished holes show the practice of trepanning. A remarkable practice was that of providing regular burials to animals. In one case five dogs were buried with antler horns. The other animal graves are of ibex, wolf and dog.

Without any stratigraphic break, the Neolithic culture ushered in Period III. Many cultural traits continue from the previous periods. Wheelmade pottery and the use of copper and even iron is evidenced. The most remarkable feature of this period is the erection of half-a-dozen massive stones (menhirs) in a semicircular fashion. Though a burial has been found below one of the menhirs, they do not contain any regular sephulchres. Burial practices otherwise are similar to those of Period II. In one case five pots were placed with the skeleton. Many grave pits of Periods II and III were dug with a narrow mouth and a wider base, in the style of the dwelling pits. A few structures of mud, a rubble wall and post-holes depict their building activity.

^{14}C Dates (T½ = 5730 years)

TF - 15	1535 ± 110 BC
TF - 129	1825 ± 100 BC
TF - 13	1850 ± 125 BC
TF - 14	2025 ± 350 BC
TF - 127	2100 ± 115 BC
TF - 123	2225 ± 115 BC
TF - 128	2375 ± 120 BC

Neolithic settlements in Kashmir are quite densely distributed. In the Jhelum valley alone, from Anantnag to Pampur, a number of sites were discovered *e.g.*, Begagund, Gufkral, Hariparigom, Jayadeviuder, Olchibag, Pampur, Panzgom, Sombur and Thajiwor. Other sites of the valley are Gurhoma Sangri, near the Wular lake and Damodara Karewa south-west of Srinagar. The sites at Aripanthan, near Magam, at Puthkah near Sangrama, Duvi-ekam-pura on way to Gulmarg are noteworthy. Gandarbal in the Sind valley and Baimlun on the Wangat Nullah were explored earlier by Paterson.

4

HUMAN BURIALS

In the northern Neolithic region of the Indian - subcontinent Burzahom occupies a unique position for revealing human and animal burials dating back to the middle of the 3rd millennium B.C. Sivalik series had the distinction to revealing richest evidences for hominid evolution. The find of Ramapithecus and its status on human origins has put India on the map of human evolution taking back the date to nearly 12 million years. As we do not have human remains of earlier than Late-Stone Age Period, the Burzahom burials assume special importance, particularly in the neolithic context. The site has yielded burials, both human and animal, belonging to neolithic and megalithic periods, all within the habitational area itself. Though another important neolithic site of Gufkral in the valley was excavated by the present author, the limited dig of two seasons could not be extended to burials, which were, as per surface indications, detected on the north-eastern corner of the sprawling mound. It appears, Gufkral had a separate cemetery area itself as large number of circular graves were found concentrated on that part of the mound.

At Burzahom, in two seasons dig, ten human and eleven animal burials were exposed, all in the habitation area itself, mostly inside the houses just below the floor. They were found at the depth of 1.25 m to 3.0 m. from the present surface. All the burials belonged to neolithic and megalithic periods. Period III *i.e.,* Early Historical period did not yield any burials. The may be due to the reason that the dig in the period was confined to a very limited area and that too to habitation deposits. It is not necessary that in the Early Historical period also the practice of burying the dead in the habitation area should continue. Evidences from other sites of this period show that there used to be distinct cemetery areas during this period. At Burzahom both human and animals were buried mostly inside carefully dug circular pits in the floor of the houses which was later on plastered. They were found to be in articulated condition. It is interesting to note that in both the cases, i.e. human and animal, the skeletons were buried in north-south orientation with skull towards north. Human burials were found as individual burials but in case of animals both individual and collective burials were practiced. In case of animals from neolithic period, it was observed that the bones were treated with red-ochre like those of the humans.

In all ten human burials were excavated (5 males, 3 females, one juvenile and one child), seven belonging to period II of the Neolithic period whereas the other three were from the megalithic period. Period I of the neolithic period, which was a circular dwelling pit period, did not yield any burials. Total abscence of burials in this period suggests that probably people of this phase practised some other mode of disposal of the dead. All the burials occur in the habitational area itself and just below the floor of the huts at a considerable depth, varying from 1.25 m to 3 ms. from the surface. The burials showed both primary and secondary internments. Almost all the skeletons were oriented north-east to south-west or north-west to south-west with skull generally towards north. They were placed in the grave pit either in crouching position (No. 2, 3, 7 & 8) or in extended position. Except skeleton Nos. 1 &6., others were buried in circular pits with their inner sides plastered with 'Chunam'. Generally the pit filling consisted of ashy material, alongwith few stone pieces. Grave goods were very scanty or totally abscent. There were five miniature pots with skeleton No. 1, a barrel shaped paste bead with skeleton No. 5, a circular soap-stone disc with three linear perforations with skeleton No. 7, and five carnelian beads in the neck region of skeleton No. 8. The skeletal remains of dog, antler, sheep and goat were deposited with the human being, at times at different levels of filling of the pit.

Period 11 : This phase yielded six internments. Interestingly both primary and secondary internments were in vogue. Common features of the burials in this phase are the occurrence of all the burials in egg-shaped oval pits. These pits had been invariably dug in the floor of the house, and were narrower towards top. All had been plastered with *Chunam* on the inner side and were of varying diameters ranging from 1' to 6'8" save in case of a child. Filling of the pit mostly consisted of ash mixed with stone pieces and pot-sherds. Animal bones were deposited along with the human internments in one case. Skulls had been placed either towards north-east or south-east, exceptions being the case of a child burial and an extended adult-burial where skulls were placed towards west.

Secondary Internments :

Out of six burials only two were secondary burials. In these secondary internments, from the postion of various bones, it appears that the skeletons must have been bare of flesh, before being placed in position. Mostly skull and long bones were collected after the process of dessication and were interred after being treated with red-ochre solution. In case of a secondary burial where the bones were treated with red ochre a peculiar feature observed was the presence of two long conical stones placed in inclining position towards the leg region on the top of the pit was dug from the depth of 1.25 m while the skeleton was lying at a depth of 1.80 m. Hands and legs were folded up at the ankle and knee points, respectively. An earthen pot filled with red ochre paste was noticed outside the pit in the same layer. The only antiquity recovered from this grave comprised of a barrel shaped paste bead.

In the second case. the skull and long bones were deposited in a cluster inside the pit after treating them with red ochre solution. Here the skull was placed toward north-east of the pit. The pit was dug at a depth of 1.27 m while the skeleton was placed at a depth of 1.65 m.

Primary Internments

In three of the burials skeletons were kept in an embryonic position in an articulated condition while in the fourth case, exceptionally, the skeleton was placed in extended position at a depth of 3.0 m. Here the orientation of the skeleton was south-west (skull) to north-east, unlike the other burials of this phase. The skull was found in a mutilated condition due to thrusting of stone pieces inside it. Incidentally the pit of this burial was dug through a dwelling pit which contained pot-shreds in profusion. Of the three primary burials in which the skeletons were placed in crouching position one was of a child hardly of 2 years' age (Pl. V-A). The grave pit of the child was noticed just beneath the left foot of a skeleton (Pl. V-B) of period III at a depth of 2.73 m. The pit was sealed by thick yellowish floor. The skull was placed towards west and the distinctly.

The second one is a case of a grown up adult (Pl. XI). Here the pit was dug at a depth of 2.8 m. The skeleton was placed at a depth of 3.10 m in south-east north-west direction resting on its left side. Five carnelian barrel beads were recovered from the neck region of the skeleton.

The third case is of striking importance. (pl. IX) Here all the bones were treated with red ochere unlike otherprimary burials. The body was kept at a depth of 2.20 mm in an oval pit in crouching position.The pit was plastered with chunam in the interior ande sealed by a yellowishfloor. The skeletonwas oriented in north - est to south-west directionresting on its right side. The most interesting features of this burial were the trephining marks on the skull. Seven finished and four unfinished holes were trepanned in the norma lateralis position on the parietal bone between bregma and lambda. None of the holes disclose any sigh of healing. They were probably made in order to obtain fatishes.[1] Some sort of surgical operation also cannot be ruled out 2 (P1 x B).

The intact condition of the bones was indicative of the fact that the red ochre solution should have been sprinkled over the skeleton after the decomposition of the flesh, thereby meaning that the burial was opened again. In the same pit fragments of animal bones particularly skull and horn pieces of antler were buried at different levels. An animal lower jaw treated with red ochre was also recovered from the same pit. The only associate antiquity was a soapstone circular flat disc. with three linear perforations.

Period III : Only three burials from this period were encountered. The occurrence of oval Chunam lined pits and the crouching position of the skeleton in one case indicate the continuation of the burial customs commonly prevalent in period II. Treatment of bones with red-ochre in this phase totally disappeared. In all probability in later years the practice of burying in Chunam lined oval pits was abandoned. The orientation of the two cases of east-west orientation in period II indicated the begining of the welcome departure of the south-east north-west orientation. Filling of the pit comprised of the pit material mixed with ash, stone pieces and potsherds. Average diameter of the oval pits was 1-35m.

---

1. De Morgan-Prehistoric Man. p. 245.
2. K.P. Okley and others-Man, Vol-LIX, 1959, No. 133, p. 93.

In one case which seems to be and accidental burial, the skull was severed from the torso and put in norma occipitalis position towards the leg region. Fragmentary bones of goat were also found from this burial.

In another case an adult male was buried in an irregular pit dug at the depth of 1.10m. The pit was tapering towards the top and was lined with stone pieces. The body was put in reclining position, resting on its back (Pl. V). It was almost in sitting at ease posture with its skull dangling over the right shoulder. It was in slanting position with the skull at a higher level (1.65m) and feet at a lower level (2.38) from the top. Five ceremonial pots had been interned along with the skeleton, of them three were placed to the right and the other two to the left of the lelft leg. No. animal bones were encountered in this grave.

In the third burial of this period an adult was buried in an oval *chunam* lined pit at a depth of 1.75m. The body of the deceased was placed on its right side in crouching position, with thw skull towards north-west. Hands and legs were in folded condition. The skull of a dog was also interned in the same pit at a depth of 0.65m from the top of the pit.

Incidentally Burzahom burials fall very much in line with the burials reported from Catal Huyuk, a neolithic site in Near East in Konya plain.[1] The burials from Tepe Hissar and Tepe Sialk[2] also reveal striking semblances with period II burials of Burzahom. The treatment of skeletons with red ochre is well-known to Russia also.

For a modern ethnological parallel we can refer to the very similar practice among the 'Paleolithic' Onge pygmies of the Andaman Isaland mentioned by Prof. Capriani.[3] The biry their dead under the floor of the hut, each being burried under his own bed.

---

1. James Mellaart in *The Illustrated London News* -February 15, 22, 1964.
2. T.J. Arne-*Excavations at Shah Tepe-Iran.*
3. Capriani in *The Illustrated London News*, February 3, 1962.

Seven days after the burial they break off the jaw bone of the deceased, paint it with red ochre and decorate it, using it as an ornament or a necklace. About three months later they exhume all the bones, wash them, paint them with ochre and bury them again in the same place. Likewise, the modern parallel of trepanning can also be drawn out from Tibu of Africa.

Basing on the facts unearthed so far and in order to trace out the cultural links to Burzahom we may have to look towards western Asia, eastern Europe and southern parts of Russia.

C. DETAILED DESCRIPTIONS

SKELETON NO. 1 (PL. V-A)

A human burial is found in the eastern extension of BZH-1 (1962) just below the eastern lateral border of the huge megalith. The grave pit is cut in layers 4, 5, 6 and 7 and sealed by layer 3 which clearly shows that the grave pit was dug earlier than the pit for the megalith. this fact is nicely expressed by the western section of trench (facing east) on which both the skull and the lower end of the megalith are resting.

The grave pit has been cut through layer 4, 5, 6, and 7. Layer 7 is actually the thick yellowish floor deposit which sealed the grave pit for the child (skeleton no.2) lying below the feet of skeleton no.1. The grave pit has been cut in a peculiar fashion and so also the skeleton has been placed. The skeleton has been placed in such a fashion that it gives an impression of a man sleeping at ease on an easy chair with his head dangling on his right shoulder. The pit is of conical shape in the section and on the plan it gradually widens from the shoulder region towards the legs. It is widest near the knees *i.e.*, 1.30m. The grave pit is narrowest near the pectoral girdle (0.45m). Actually at this point the pit has narrowed down to such an extent that its edges are just touching the right humerus on one side and the left ribs on the other.

The top of layer 7 on which the back of the skeleton is resting consists of burnt floor.

The skeleton is lying or say reclining from west to east with its skull towards west facing south-east and the left leg towards east. The right leg is bent at the knee point and the lower ends of right tibia and fibula are just below the condylar region of the left femur. On the left side *i.e.*, the northern corner of the pit, the pit has been lined by fairly big stone pieces. The left foot is between the two big stones lying just over the child's (skeleton no. 2) skull.

Five miniature earthen goblets are found inside the grave pit associated with the skeleton. Three of the pots are put in a triangular fashion on the right of the left leg while two are on the left side of the same leg. The skeleton as a whole is slightly bent towards the right from the pelvis region above. The skeleton was first exposed in the year 1961 but neither it could be treated chemically nor could be lifted and has to be covered with earth again due to shortage of time and inclement weather. Heavy incrustation has taken place on the bones and some of the parts namely the skull and the pelvis region are damaged.

The top of the grave is at the depth of 1.10m from the present surface level while the top of the skull is at the depth of 1.68m. The pelvis region is at the depth of 2.10m and the left feet is at the depth of 2.38m.

The skeleton is in articulated condition lying on its back.

Skull:- (Pls. VIA & B)The occipital region and the right parietal bones of the skull are lying inside the western section facing east. The skull is bent slightly towards right with the chin resting on the right shoulder. Except for the damage in the nasal and the right orbital regions the skull is in fairly good state of preservation. It is hollow from inside.

Frontal bone is in good condition except for a crack running parallel to the coronal suture. The coronal suture is complete and do not show any remarkable sign of fusion. Frontal bone is curved and the forehead is receeding. Eye-brow ridges are prominent. Upper margins of the orbits of the eyes are not sharp. Glabella is prominent.

Fortunately the nasal bone is intact. Superciliary arch is prominent and so also the frontal tubercle. Zygomatic bones on both the sides are intact. Though the left zygomatic process is complete, the zygomatic bone is displaced from the maxilla due to break between the junction of upper process of maxilla and the frontal bone and at the point of infraorbital foramen. The right zygomatic bone has also got pressed inside the orbit. The muscular ridges on the frontal bone are well developed. Frontal process of right maxilla is missing. Anterior nasal spine is present. All the eight teeth of the left maxilla are intact including the left maxillary tuberosity.

Left parietal bone is intact and in good state of preservation. It has also developed a crack running throughout the length of the bone, roughly parallel to the sagittal suture.

Left temporal bone is intact. Squamous part, mastoid portion, zygomatic process, parietal notch, articular tubercle, mandibular fossa, suprameatal triangle, and the mastoid process, all are intact and in good condition. Mastoid process is quite prominent. Greater wing of sphenoid bone on the left side is present. Left orbital plate of ethmoid is broken near the greater wing of sphenoid bone.

Mandible is more or less intact with the chin resting on acromial end of the right clavicle. Mandible is broken into two halves. Head and coronoid process are intact in the left half of the mandible which is exposed. Angle, mental foramen and mental protuberance, all are intact. All the eight teeth of the left side and the two incisors of the right side are visible in articulated condition. Jaw bone is rough with well developed marks of muscular attachments.

Bones of the skull are quite thick.

Clavicle:- Both the clavicles are intact and in proper articulated condition. Right one is broken at its acromial end while the deltoid region and the sternal ends are complete. Left clavicle is slightly damaged at the sternal end. Both are very fragile.

Scapula:- Major portion of both the scapulae are still inside the section. Acromian and coracoid process of the left scapula are partly visible.

Ribs:- Nearly all the ribs are represented either completely or by fragments. As most of the ribs are riding over each other, on the right side twelve are visible while on the left only six are intact but they are so fragile that it is doubtful as to how much can be lifted intact.

Vertebral column:- The vertebral column is more or less complete with nearly all the vertebrae present though in extremely fragile and broken condition. Atlas, axis, cervical, thoracic and lumbar all are present. Facets of the body are damaged while the spines are hardly present except in few. All the five sacral vertebrae with their foramen of the right side are present. On the left side foramen of only first and second are present. Lateral part of the sacrum on the right side is intact while that of the left side is broken. Coccyx are missing.

Just above the right pelvic bone between the right ribs and the lumbar vertebrae, are lying the manubrium and the first segment of the sternum. They are extremely fragile and are disturbed from their proper place. The supra sternal notch is intact while the socket for the first coastal cartilage is damaged.

Humerus I:- Both the humerii are intact in proper articulated condition. The hands are in stretched position with the right forearm slightly bent towards the pelvis and passing over the right femur.

Left humerus is complete. Shaft and lower ends of both the humerii are intact and complete except for that of the upper end of the shaft of the left humerus which is broken. Head of the left humerus is complete while that of the right is damaged near the lesser tubercle. Surgical and anatomical neck and greater tubercle of both are intact. Coracoid fossa, radial fossa, trochlea, capitulum and epicondyles of both are intact. Lateral and medial supra condylar ridges of both are in good conditions.

Fore-arms:- Both the fore-arms are in articulated condition. Right fore-arm is slightly bent towards the pelvis and is twisted in such a fashion that the head of radius is over-riding the olecranon process of ulna. Except for slight damages on the surface of distal and proximal ends both the ulnae are complete. Olecranon process, trochlear notch, coracoid process, shaft and head are intact. Similarly both the radii are in good state of preservation. Left radius is broken into two at the lower end of its shaft. Head neck, biceps and styloid process are intact.

Carpus, metacarpus and phalanges:- Hand and wrist bones are not in full extension. They are in slightly bent position, right towards the innerside, while the left towards the outer side. Almost all the carpal and metacarpal bones and phalanges are present and are in good state of preservation.

Pelvis:- Ventral aspect of pelvis is visible in in-situ condition. Unfortunately most of the bones are damaged and are in extremely decomposed condition. Crest and margins of both the ilium are missing. Anterior superior and anterior inferior spines are in damaged condition. The auricular surfaces and greater sciatic notches are intact. Acetabular cavity of the left hip bone is more or less completely missing while that of the right side is present. Pubic bones of both the sides including the pubic symphyses are totally absent. Body and ramus of ischiatic bones are present in damaged and broken condition. Tuberosities and spines are present.

Pelvic cavity and sciatic notches are narrow and deep. Sacrum is quite big in size. Auricular surface of the sacrum extends upto the middle of third vertebrae. Acetabulae are quite big, deep and close to each other.

Femur:- Both the thigh bones are in articulated condition with their heads properly lodged in their respective acetabular cavities. Left leg is lying in full flexed condition while the right is bent at the knee. Anterior aspect of the left while the lateral aspect of the right femur is visible. Head of both the femurii are extremely fragile. Head of the left femur is damaged but the greater and lesser trochanter are intact. Neck is also slightly damaged. Head of right femur is intact along with the lesser trochanter. Shaft and distal ends of both the femurii are intact. Heavy encrustration has taken place particularly on the shaft of left femur. Condyles and patellar surface of left femur is intact. Medial and lateral condyles of the right femur are in damaged condition. Patellar surface is in considerably good condition.

Patella:- Both the patella are in their proper articulated condition. The three borders and the apex are intact along with the muscular markings.

Tibia:- Both the leg bones are in their articulated condition. Frontal aspect of the left leg is visible while the lateral aspect of the right.

Left tibia is intact in its upper, middle and lower regions. Right tibia is slightly damaged at the point of medial condyle. Tubercles, lateral condyles, anterior and medial surfaces of the shaft and medial malleolus of both the tibiable are in good condisiton.

Fibula:- Both the fibulae are in articulated condition with their head, apex and lateral malleolus intact. The left fibula is broken into two at the middle of the shaft.

Foot bones:- Tarsal and metatarial bones and phalanges of both the feet are in good condition. Right foot bones are firmly intact but the left ones are disturbed from their position as the left foot is lying between two big stones. Calcaneus, talus, cuneiform and other tarsus and metatarsus are complete but some of the phalanges of the left foot are missing.

MEASUREMENT IN-SITU CONDITION

1. Length of humerus (Right) = 33.5 cms
2. Length of humerus (Left) = 33.5 cms
3. Length of radius (Right) = 25.8 cms
4. Length of radius (Left) = 25.9 cms
5. Length of ulna (Right) = 26.0 cms
6. Length of ulna (Left) = 26.0 cms
7. Length of femur (Right) = 45.6 cms

8. Length of Femur (Left) = 45.5 cms
9. Length of Tibia (Right) = 37.5 cms
10. Length of Tibia (Left) = 37.6 cms
11. Length of Fibula (Right) = 37.8 cms
12. Length of Fibula (Left) = 37.8 cms
13. Maxium distance between pelvis plate = 28.5 cms

The skeleton belongs to that of an adult male of nearly fifty years of age.

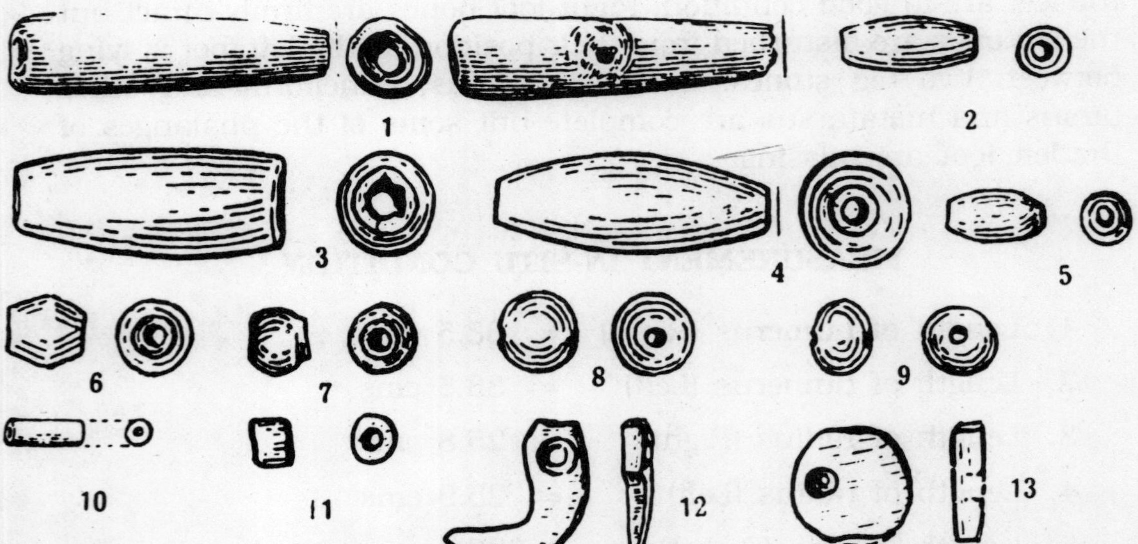

SKELETON NO. 2 (Pl. V-B)

A skeleton of a baby is found in a grave pit below the left foot of skeleton No. 1 in the area BZH-1(62), eastern extension, just below the eastern edge of the megalith. Top of the grave pit is at the depth of 2.73m from the present ground level. The thick yellowish floor sealing the grave-pit and marked as layer 7, has been disturbed on the western side by the grave-pit of skeleton No. 1.

The skeleton was detected through the top of its skull which got exposed while cleaning the two big stone pieces lying below the left foot of skeleton No. 1. The stone on the northern side is directly lying over the skull of the child and it is just likely that while digging the pit for skeleton No. 1 the diggers came across the child's skull and in order not to disturb it they just protected it by putting two stones over it and laid the body of their own deceased.

The maximum available length of the child's grave pit is 0.70m (east-west) and maximum breadth from north to south is 0.75m. The filling of the pit consists of black clay with three stone pieces placed on its western border lining the pit.

The skeleton is lying in foetal position from west to east with the skull towards west facing north. Hands and feet have been folded to a considerable extent and have been placed in such a way that the right hand is lying over the left foot and the left hand below the left foot. The skeleton is resting on its left side. Maximum available length of the skeleton in in-situ condition from the top of the skull to the pubic region is 0.40m.

Skull:- The skull is resting on its left side in an inclined position just below the left foot of skeleton No. 1. Fortunately the vault is safe but the face along with the mandible is badly damaged. Nasal bone is completely missing. Frontal, temporal, parietal and occipital bones are more or less intact. The skull bones are very smooth and thin. Except for a part of right coronal suture and right temporal suture other sutures are not visible due to the stone lying above the skull. A part of the frontal bone just above the pterion point is missing. Fore-head is narrow and smooth. Supra-orbital notch along with the upper borders of both the eye orbits are intact. Right mastoid process and external acoustic meatus are in good condition. Greater wing of right sphenoid as well as the squamous temporal are in good state of preservation. Frontal process of maxilla of both the sides are completely missing. Zygomatic bone with zygomatic process of right side is absent. Nasal spine is missing. Left zygomatic bone is present. Only infra-orbital foramen is present.

The margin of right orbit below supra-orbital foramen to fronto-zygomatic suture is missing. Galbella is intact.

Only the right half of the mandible is exposed. Ramus and the condylar process with the head of mandible is intact, but the coronoid process is slightly damaged at the end. Angle is safe. Except for 1st molar all other teeth are missing. Mandible had broken into two pieces at the point of mental protuberance. Second permanent molar tooth has erupted but is missing.

Vertebral Column and Ribs:- Nearly all the vertebrae are present in disarticulated condition with most of them devoid of their spines. As the child is lying in crouching position the vertebral column is also in curved position. Right half of the pectoral girdle is superimposed over the left half. Cervical vertebrae are not visible. Nearly all the ribs of the right side are visible, at least eight of them and are mostly broken and fragile. Ribs of the left side are hidden by those of the right side.

Scapula:- Right scapula is lying more or less in its proper place. Deltoid process is broken while the glenoid cavity and supra-scapular notch is intact. Scapular plate, lateral and medial borders are also intact. Inferior angle is in good condition.

Clavicle:- Right clavicle is lying just below the deltoid process of the right scapula. Its acromial and sternal ends are more or less intact.

Humerus:- Both the upper and lower limb bones are lying bundled up parallel to each other. Only right humerus is visible and is in slightly disturbed condition. Head is damaged and disturbed from its glenoid cavity. Anatomical neck is intact. Olecranon fossa is developed but the lateral and medial epicondyles as well as the trochlea are not at all properly developed. On the whole the bone is in fairly good condition.

Fore-arm and Hand bones:- Right radius and ulna are present but lying just near the left femur. Their extremities are damaged and both are in extremely fragile condition. Ossification is not yet complete at the upper ends. All the five metacarpals of the right hand are present. They are very tiny and delicate. Carpal bones are not visible. Left radius and ulna are lying below the temporal bone and are only partly visible.

Hip bone:- Only the Iliac portion of the right hip bone is visible and is in articulated condition. The crest is intact and fortunately the iliac portion is not damaged. Right pubic bone is also intact along with its acetabular cavity which is very shallow. Anterior superior spine and posterior inferior spine of the ilium are intact.

Left hip bone is badly damaged. Only the ilium is visible which is crushed into several pieces and hardly anything can be lifted. Both the hip bones are extremely delicate and fragile.

Femur:- Right femur is in articulated condition and is complete. Head is intact and so also the neck which is only slightly developed. Lesser trochanter had not developed and the greater trochanter is in the process of appearance. Shaft is smooth and intact. Lateral condyle is slightly developed and delicate.

Left femur is also in articulated condition with the head inside the acetabular cavity. Greater trochanter is in the process of appearance while the lesser is not at all developed. Lower end is damaged. Shaft is intact. Lateral and medical condyles are partly present.

Tibia:- Right tibia is lying parallel to the right femur as the legs have been folded. View of upper end is obstructed by the lower end of right femur. Only a part of lower end is visible. Shaft is intact.

Left tibia is only partly visible as it is lying below the bones of the right arm. It is more or less complete with some damages at the extremities.

Fibula:- Right fibula has broken into two from the centre of the shaft. Its head, shaft and lateral malleolus are intact. Ossification is complete in the shaft. At the lower end it is in comparatively advanced stage while at the upper end it has just started

Left fibula is lying below the right radius and ulna and is thus not visible.

Patella:- Both the right and left patella are in their proper position. They are extremely delicate and fragile. Ossification has already made its appearance.

Foot bones:- Only two metatarsal bones are lying near the right patella while the rest are missing.

The skeleton is that of a child of nearly five to six years of age.

SKELETON NO. 3

A human skeleton resting on its right side and burried in crouching position was found in a grave pit in the area BZH-1, Vx'-VIIx'. Major portion of the pit is on the plan while a little is inside the eastern section (looking east) of the trench. The pit had been cut in layer 3a sealed by layer 3. Top of the pit is at the depth of 0.70m from the present surface level. Maximum available length of the grave pit on the plan at the level where the skeleton is lying is 1.35m, while the maximum breadth on the plan is 0.50m.

Along with the human skeleton is burried a skull of a dog (probably) in the pit at the depth of 0.65m from the top of the pit and is projecting from the section looking east. Human skeleton is lying at the depth of 1.05m from the top of the pit. Skull of the dog (?) is just above the left hip-bone and is in badly damaged condition. Facial parts are totally missing. Sagittal crest is quite prominent. One canine from the lower jaw is visible. The skull is lying submerged amongst big stone pieces and a considerable part of it is still inside the section and thus it cannot be said at present whether there is a complete skeleton or only the skull.

Pit-filling can be divided into three distinct deposits. Top deposit consists of black soil mixed with stone pieces. Material of the middle deposit is made up of layers 6 and 7 through which the pit has been cut. It is compact soil mixed with *chunam* pieces. The lowest deposit consists of loose ashy material mixed with numerous stone pieces. A clear *chunam* lining on the northern side of the pit is visible, while the same is not traceable on the southern side of the pit. Actually the scalp touches the *chunam* plastering.

The human skeleton is lying on the north western side of the pit extending from north-west to south-east, with the skull towards north-west facing south and the pelvis towards south-east.

The skeleton has been folded so much to bring it in the foetal position that its length is reduced to 0.63m measured from the crown to the pubic crest. From the position of the legs it seems that they might have been folded and tied with a string to the back of the

Owner before the body was buried. Fore-limbs were also in folded condition with right-hand bones lying below the right ear.

Skull :

The Skull was resting on its right side facing towards south-east. It was in badly damaged condition and had broken into several pieces. Frontal, parietal, temporal and occipţal rigions, all had broken into several pieces. Coronal and sagittal sutures were clearly visible and had not fused. Maxilla was broken into several pieces. Last mastoid process was prominent and porion points were intact. Left zygomatic process was also more or less intact except for slight displacement at the suture where it joins the zygomatic bone. Frantal process of maxilla was also broken. Nasal bone though intact had separated from the frontal bone and frontal process of Maxilla on both the sides. Left orbit had got damaged near the supra orbital foramen which was visible. Right orbit was not visible. Only tow incisors, one canine and one premolar of the left side of the upper jaw were visible. Anterior nasal spine was missing. Left occipital bone was also not visible due to 'Chunam' lining. Squamous part of the left temporal bone was present. Only the left condylar process of the mandible was visible as the rest of parts were obscued by the left humerus which passed over the mandible. Condylar process was broken into three pieces. Bones of the skull were quite thick and sutures had not at all fused. Teeth did not show any marked sign of wear and tear.

Vertebrae and ribs :

Only an impression of the vertebral coumn was left. All the verteberae were in very much decomposed condition. Vertebrae column was much curved as the whole body was kept in crouching position. Vetebrae were very profile with spinous process of most of them broken. First and other five ribs of the left side were present but had broken at several points. Shaft portion of the five ribs of the right side were present. None of the clavricle was visible.

Scapula :

Both the scapulae were only partly exposed and were represented by fragments in extreme delicate conditions. Acromian and coracoid process of the right scapula was in damaged condition. Glenoid cavity alongwith the lateral border of the spine of the left scapula was visible.

Acromion and coracoid cavity along with the lateral border of the spine of the left scapula is visible.

Humerus:- Both the humerii are more or less in articulated condition. From the right humerus only a portion of the lower part of the shaft with medial epicondyle is to be seen. Shaft is broken. Left humerus is more or less completely exposed except for its distal end which is hidden by the shaft of the left femur. Head of the left humerus is broken into several pieces above the surgical neck and is extremely fragile. Shaft has also broken into two pieces at the point of deltoid tuberosity.

Radius and Ulna:- Due to the folded condition of the hands none of the fore-arm bones are visible except for a small portion of the upper end of the right ulna which seems to be in good condition. The left fore-arm seems to be passing below the distal end of the left femur and right maxilla. Skull seems to be resting on the left palm as two phalanges are lying just below the scalp of the skull. Four phalanges of the right hand are lying near the cervical region of the vertebral column. Styloid process of the right radius is visible near the coracoid process of the right scapula.

Hip-Bones: The body is resting over the right hip-bone. Pelvis is in proper articulated condition. Only the left half of pelvis is exposed and is in fairly good condition though damaged at several points. External surface of the left iliac bone has cracked into several pieces. Iliac crest is quite intact. Anterior superior spine and posterior inferior spine, both are intact. Left acetabular cavity is in good condition with the head of the left femur lodged in it. Transverse and longitudinal ridges of the tuberosity of left ischium, are slightly damaged along with the left pubic syphysis. Right pubic symphysis is in better condition. Spine of left ischium is present. Bones of the pelvis are strong with well marked muscle impressions. Curves of the iliac crest are will pronounced. Depth of pubic symphysis is considerable. Margins of the pubic arch are everted. Acetabulum is quite big.

Femur: Both the femurii are quite intact and in articulated condition. Lower limbs have been folded considerably. Knees have been brought near thigh. Upper end of the left femur is in good condition with its head lodged in the acetabular cavity. Head and neck are intact but the greater trochanter is damaged. Lesser trochanter is not visible. The shaft is intact except at its lower end where it has cracked into several pieces at the supra condylar point. At the lower end the medial condyle is damaged and is extremely fragile. Maximum available length of left femur in 39.7 cms.

Right femur is also in fairly good condition. Only the neck is visible. Shaft has cracked into pieces at its lower third. Gluteal tuberosity is quite intact. Popliteal surface is also intact, but the medial and lateral condyles are damaged. Inter condylar fossa is in better condition.

Tibia and Fibula: Only the upper half of the left tibia is present. It is fragile and has broken into several pieces. Medial condyle is slightly damaged. Shaft is broken. Right leg bones are totally missing. Upper two third of the left fibula is present, below left femur with its shaft in broken condition. Head is intact. Both the patella are present. Left patella is in its proper place while the right is lying between the upper end of the left femur and the lower end of left humerus.

Foot bones are completely missing.

The skeleton belongs to a female of about 30 to 35 years of age.

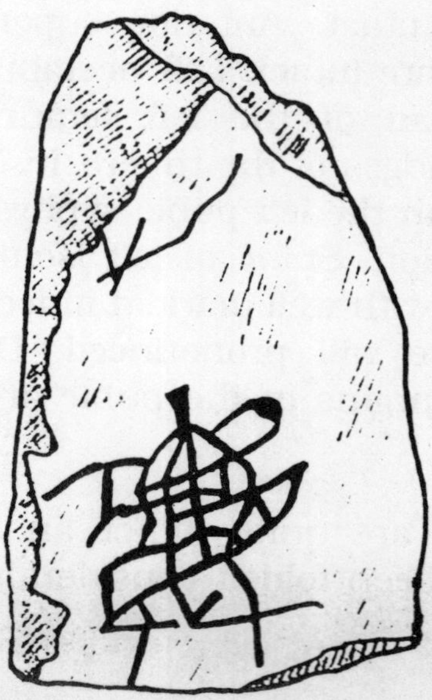

SKELETON NO. 4

A human skeleton was found in a grave pit in the trench BZH-3 (62) between peg Nos. XX and XVII. The grave pit has been cut in layer 5 and is sealed by layer 4b. It is situated just near the southern section of the trench. At the first instance a part of the pit occurred inside the section looking south and thus in order to expose the pit completely on the plan, this section was pushed back. From the present ground level top of the pits was at the depth of 1.275m while the skeleton at the depth of 1.65m, and at the depth of 0.50m from the top of the grave pit.

None of the bones are in proper articulation. Actually it is a case of typical secondary burial in which various parts of the human skeleton have been collected and put inside the pit after the body was exposed to the atmosphere. All the bones available have been treated with red-ochre.

The grave-pit is oval in shape, narrower towards the top and wider towards the bottom. It is filled with ashy deposits mixed with stone pieces. It is plastered by *chunam* all along its inner borders. Maximum length of the pit (east-west) is 1.15m while maximum breadth where the skeleton is lying is 0.825m. The skeleton is lying in east-west direction with the skull towards north east corner of the pit.

Skull:- Skull along with the mandible is resting on its right side facing south east. Red ochre from the exposed side of the skull is washed away as this part was first exposed in the year 1961. During the previous season whole of the skeleton could not be exposed due to paucity of time and the exposed parts were left covered with loose earth. The skull has cracked into numerous fragments. Atleast twenty two pieces are visible on the exposed side. Frontal bone is quite intact though broken. Skull has become flattish and long due to pressure. Left parietal and temporal bones have broken into several pieces. Actually major cracks have developed all along the left side of the coronal suture, sagittal suture and left lambdoid suture. Left mastoid process is completely missing but the left porion point is intact. Only the left maxilla is visible and is represented by at least four pieces. Left zygmatic bone is badly damaged and extremely fragile.

Neither the nasal bones nor the eye-orbits are visible. Frontal process of maxilla is also not visible in in-situ condition. Three molars, two pre-molars, and one canine of the left maxilla are visible. Left mandible is badly damaged. Head of the mandible, coronoid process and the portion above the angle are missing. Only a small portion with three molars and one pre-molar is left.

A fragment of left clavicle is present. Left scapula is in badly damaged condition and is extremely fragile.

Limb Bones

Most of the limb bones have been collected and kept bundled up to-gether. It contains femur tibia and fibula of both the sides, the two patella, pieces of radius and ulna from both the sides and one humerus. Lower and upper extremeties of all these bones are in badly damaged condition. They are very fragile. Tarsus and metatarsus bones are in more or less articulated condition with their respective leg bones. Some of the phalanges of the hands are lying scattered between the bones of the hind limbs. All the bones have been nicely treated with red-ochre.

Except for the bones described above all other parts are completely missing *e.g.*, pelvis, ribs, vertebral column etc.

Though the size of the skull is quite big, limb bones are fairly small and delicate. Eruption of all the teeth is completed. Fore-head is narrow. The skeleton seems to be that of a juvenile aged around 15 years.

In the lower jaw three molars have erupted and most probably the wisdom teeth have also erupted and are hidden. None of the sutures have fused.

SKELETON NO. 5 (Pl. VII)

Remains of human skeleton treated with red ochre is found in an egg shaped (in longitudinal section) grave-pit plastered all around its inner sides by *chunam*. The grave prit is in south-eastern quadrant of square B. I. in area BZH-3 (1961). From the condition of the bones it seems that after the decomposition of the flesh, the skeleton was exposed again and red-ochre solution was sprinkled over the remains.

Grave-pit has been cut in layer 6 at the depth of 1.25m from the present surface level and is sealed by layer 5. Bottom of the pit where the skeleton is lying is at the depth of 1.80m B.S. Two long and sharp stones inclining towards south-east, were buried on the top of the pit. Incidentally after scooping the western half of the pit, skull was found lying in south-eastern corner of the pit. Legs were found on the northern side of the pit, exactly in the same direction where the burried ends of the stones were pointing.

The pit is roughly 0.55m deep. It has disturbed four earlier pits cut into natural soil. The quadrant contains as many as eight pits on the plan, all plastered by *'chunam'* on their inner sides. The highest point of the skeleton is lying at the depth of 0.35m from the top of the pit. The skeleton is lying in north south direction with its skull towards south-eastern corner. Though it seems to be a case of secondary burial but most of the parts are in articulated condition. Both the upper and lower limbs are in folded condition. All the bones below pelvis region are lying on the natural soil itself.

The grave pit is more or less a perfect circle with a diameter of 1.60m at the bottom though it was less at the top as the pit is broader at the bottom and narrower at the top. Maximum length of the skeleton in in-situ condition from the skull vault to the lower extremity of the femur is 1.20m. Roughly, the top of the iliac crest is in the centre of the pit.

Skull:- Skull is resting on its right side in an extremely damaged condition. Actually some of the facial bones are not at all visible. Temporal piece has separated from the parietal bone of left side.

Occipital and parietal bones have cracked into several pieces and are extremely fragile. The external occipital protuberance is facing west.

Temporal piece of the left side is not at all present. Eye orbits, nasal bones and the zygomatic processes are, completely missing. Twelve teeth are lying scattered near the occipital bone and the frontal bone. Mandible is reduced to tiny fragments and hardly anything can be lifted.

Only a piece of right scapula is present. It has cracked into several pieces. Glenoid cavity is in fairly good condition while both the acromion and coracoid process are abscent. Infra glenoid tubercle is present and rest of the portions below it are missing.

Left scapula is damaged from several points and is extremely fragile. Spine along with the acromion process is intact but the coracoid process is broken. Glenoid cavity is fitted with very fragile humerous head. Superior and inferior angles of the scapula are missing. Lateral border of the scapula is broken whereas the plate is extremely fragile. One tooth is lying near left scapula.

Both the clavicles are missing.

Hardly anything more than the impression of the ribs is left and nothing worth study can be lifted.

Humerus

Both the hands have been folded with the palms coming near the skull and are in more or less articulated condition. Head and greater tubercle of right humerus are missing. Only the portion below the surgical neck is present and has broken from several places, particularly at the proximal end of the shaft. At the distal end shaft has cracked near the lateral supra condylar ridge. Olecranon fossa, lateral epicondyle, medial epicondyle and trochlea are in fairly good state of preservation.

Head of left humerus is damaged and extremely fragile. It is lying inserted inside the glenoid cavity. Proximal end below the lateral supra-condylar ridge is badly damaged and fragile. Shaft is in fairly good condition.

Radius and Ulna

Right fore-arm bones are in articulated condition and running parallel to the right humerus. Ulna has broken into three major pieces but is in fairly good condition. Olecranon, trochlear notch and head of the ulna, are intact except for the coracoid process which is slightly damaged, Head and neck of the radius are intact. It has broken below the radial tuberosity. Styloid process and portion below it have broken into several pieces and it is extremely difficult to lift them intact. Rest of the shaft is in fairly good state of preservation.

Left radius and ulna are badly damaged and extremely fragile. Neither the distal nor the proximal ends of any are present. Hardly anything can be lifted intact.

A small barrel shaped paste bead is lying between the left humerus and left radius. Only earth impressions of two or three vertebrae are visible while the whole of the vertebral column has disintegrated.

Hip Bones

Bones from the left hand are completely missing while a few of them from the right hand are lying scattered and broken near the styloid process of the right radius.

Pelvic region is represented only by a piece of left iliac bone. It has cracked into numerous pieces and is extremely fragile. Right hip bone has completely disintegrated.

Legs are also lying in folded condition as the fore-arms. Both the legs have been folded in such a fashion that right foot bones are riding over the left foot bones and both are lying near the left hip-bone. Actually right calcaneus is lying over the left hip bone itself.

Femur

Right femur has broken into several pieces but is lying in articulated condition. Head, neck, greater and lesser trochanteric regions are damaged and only an impression is left. Shaft below the lesser trochanteric region is broken into several pieces. Popliteal surface is in fairly good condition while the lateral and medial condyles are broken and fragile.

Left femur has also broken into several pieces. Portion above the middle of the shaft is represented by only few fragments. Head and neck are completely missing. Region below the popliteal surface is badly damaged.

Both the patella are missing.

Tibia and Fibula

Right tibia has broken in the centre and the lower end is missing. Medial and lateral condyles as well as the tubercles are in fairly good condition. Right fibula has also broken into several pieces except for the head.

Left tibia is reduced to numerous fragments. Upper end and condylar region are in fairly good condition, as compared to the lower end which is completely damaged at the malleolus region. Only one or two pieces from left fibula are left.

Foot Bones

Right calcaneous and talus bones are extremely fragile and have cracked into several pieces. All the five metatarsals of the right foot are present in pieces.

Left calcaneus is in articulated condition with its lateral and medial tubercles damaged. Talus, cuboid and cuneiform bones are hidden below the metatarsals of the right side. All the five metatarsals are present along with the phalanges.

Limb bones on the whole are of considerable length and quite sturdy.

All the bones present are dull red as they have been treated with red-ochre. Red ochre from the exposed side of the skull and right hand has been washed away as these parts were exposed in the year 1961 also.

An earthen pot was found in the north eastern corner outside the grave-pit in layer 6. Lot of red-ochre is adhering on the inner side of the pot which shows that red-ochre solution was kept in it.

The skeleton belongs to a male aged between 50 to 55 years.

BURZAHOM
(KASHMIR)
SCHEMATIC SECTION

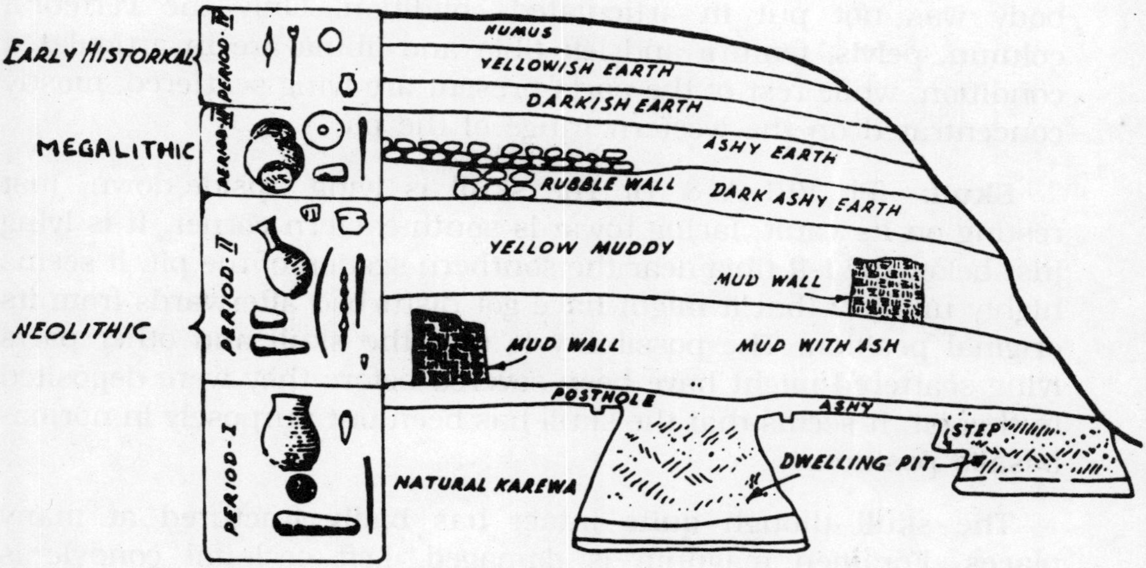

SKELETON NO. 6

Remains of a human skeleton along with some animal bones were found in a slit cut in the eastern section of the jeep track. Proximal end of right femur and a portion of right hip bone were spotted along with the grave-pit line in the section, while constructing an approach road to the site. Later on a slit was cut in the eastern section to expose the skeleton. At present the trench has been left unstratified. A pit has been cut at *'chunam'* flooring level which lies at the depth of 0.725m from the present surface level. The pit is slightly oval shaped though its western end has been cut while making the jeep track. Maximum available length of the pit from east to west is 1.675m. and maximum breadth north to south is 1.425m. The skeletal remains are lying on the western fringe of the pit, in north south direction at the depth of 0.40m from the top of the pit. The pit is filled with numerous stone pieces and ashy material.

The position of various parts give an impression that the whole body was not put in articulated condition. Only the vertebral column, pelvis, femurii and left tibia and fibula are in articulated condition, while rest of the parts present are lying scattered, mostly concentrated on the western fringe of the pit.

Skull:- (Pl. VIII A & B) The skull is lying upside-down, just resting on its vault, facing towards south-eastern corner. It is lying just below the left tibia near the southern section of the pit. It seems highly unlikely that it might have got disturbed afterwards from its original position. The possibility is that the skull and other parts lying scattered might have been severed before they were deposited in this pit. It seems that the skull has been put purposely in norma-basalis position.

The skull though quite intact has badly fractured at many places. Foramen magnum is damaged. Left occipital condyle is intact and the right one is damaged. Parietal bone is separated from the occipital pieces at the lambdoid suture. Left half of the parietal bone is missing. Left mastoid process is quite intact while the right one is badly damaged. Styloid process, pharyngeal tubercle and posterior nasal spine all are missing. Zygomatic bone along with the zygomatic process of both the sides are intact though the left zygomatic process has broken into three pieces. Palatine process of maxilla is represented by several small fragments and neither the median palatine suture nor the palato-maxillary suture is visible. All the sixteen teeth of the upper jaw are intact. Left incisor is slightly damaged. Most of them are much worn out.

Left temporal is pressed inside. Anterior aspect of the skull is more or less intact though fractured into several pieces. Both the eye-orbits are present. Upper ridge of the right orbit is broken at the supra-orbital foramen and the outer piece is pressed inside the orbit. Glabella region is present but nasion and nasal bone, both are missing. Basion point is fairly intact. Frontal process of maxilla is present with the infra-orbital foramen intact. All the bones are very fragile.

Lower jaw is totally missing.

Skull walls are quite thick. Glabella and mastoid process are prominent. Upper margins of the orbits are not so sharp. Skull vault is arched and facial bones are rough. The skull seems to be that of a male aged between 50 to 55 years. Wisdom teeth have erupted, cusps of the molars are worn out. Sagittal suture is markedly fused and so also the coronal suture. Temporal and lambdoid sutures have not fused.

Vertebra

Vertebral column is present only below the fifth thoracic vertebra. 8th thoracic vertebra is also missing. All the cervical and six thoracic vertebrae are missing. Spinous process of most of them are missing.

Hip-Bones

Right hip bone has broken into several pieces and extremely fragile, particularly the right ilium. Left iliac bone is in fairly good condition. Pubic region is also damaged particularly in the region of pubic symphysis. Ischiatic portion is not clearly visible.

Femur; Tibia and Fibula

Heads of both the femurii are lodged in their respective acetabular cavities. Both the femurii have been placed in crossed position at their lower extremeties. Left femur is broken into several pieces at its lower and upper ends. Shaft is intact. Head is extremely fragile and hardly anything intact can be lifted. At the distal end it is broken at the popliteal surface. Patellar surface is intact, Medial condyle is broken.

Right femur is in more damaged condition than the left one. Head has cracked from the point of lesser to the greater trochanter. Shaft has also broken into several pieces. Lower extremity has broken into several pieces and is extremely fragile, below the popliteal surface. Right tibia and fibula have been folded in such a fashion that their distal ends are touching the region of pubic symphysis. Left femur is passing over the right leg bones. Right tibia is intact at its upper and lower extremeties but the shaft is broken into several longitudinal pieces. Condyles and tubercles are safe. Only the lower half of the right fibula is visible which is in good condition along with the head. Upper half is lying under the left femur.

Left leg bones are considerably damaged. Left tibia is broken into three pieces at its lower end. Medial condyle is damaged. Lateral condyle, tubercles and medial malleolus are intact. Only the lower half of the left fibula is visible while the view of upper half is obstructed by the skull. Lateral malleolus and shaft, are broken.

Rest of the bones are lying scattered.

Humerus

Left humerus is broken at the distal end. It is lying in such a fashion that its distal end is riding over the head of the left pubic bone. Head is slightly damaged. Shaft is broken into pieces at the lower end. Olecranon fossa and posterior aspect of trochlea are intact. Medial and lateral condyles are damaged. In the interior aspect, coronoid fossa, medial and lateral condyles and the capitulum are completely damaged.

Only the lower half of the right humerus is present, lying crossed below the left humerus. Coronoid fossa, trochlea and the capitulum are intact, while the condyles are damaged.

Radius and Ulna

An ulna (probably the right) is lying near the left humerus. its head, shaft and trochlear notch are intact. Olecranon and coronoid process are damaged. Shaft of another ulna is lying near the right tibia.

Left radius is complete and is lying between the skull and right ulna. Its head, shaft, neck and styloid process are intact.

Right radius is lying below the left femur and pelvic bone with only head and neck visible. Both the scapulae are present but are so fragile that hardly anything can be lifted. Left scapula has cracked into several pieces. Glenoid cavity is intact but the coracoid process and the angles are badly damaged.

Only the glenoid cavity of the right scapula which is lying below the left femur is visible. Left humerus head is more or less in articulated condition.

A rib fragment is lying near the left radius and a clavicle shaft is lying near the left scapula.

Five fragments of animal bones are lying along with this human skeleton. A piece of scapula near the left radius, one radius piece near the rib, lower half of humerus by the side of left tibia, a shaft piece and a cannon bone, are lying mixed.

The animal bones seem to belong to a goat.

The skeleton belongs to that of a male aged between 50 to 55 years.

SKELETON NO. 7 (Pl. IX)

A grave pit is found in the north western sector of quadrant C. 8, in the area BZH-3 (1962). The pit has been cut in the floor (*chunam*) level termed as layer 5 and sealed by layer 4. The pit filling consists of ashy material and stone pieces. The pit has been plastered by *'chunam'* on all its inner sides. The pit is egg shaped in section, narrower towards the top and widening towards the bottom. After scooping out the filling of the pit a badly damaged skull piece and horn pieces of an autler were found at the depth of 1.83m below the present surface level. A fragment of animal lower jaw treated with red-ochre was also found near the skull. After removing the above mentioned bones the pit was further scooped and at the depth of 2.10m below the surface level more antler horn pieces were found.

After removing the horn pieces the pit was further scooped out and at the depth of 2.20m, a human skeleton burried in crouching position is found. Major part of the pit has been traced on the plan except for a small portion which is still inside the western section. Approximate diameter of the pit at the level where the human skeleton is lying is 1.20m.

The skeleton is lying north-east to south-west with the skull towards the former and pelvis towards the later direction. It is facing west. Legs and hands have been folded to a considerable extent. All the parts are in extremely fragile condition and some of them have decomposed so much that only their impression on the soil is left.

All the parts available are brick red in colour as they have been treated with red-ochre after the flesh was removed.

It seems that the skeleton was exposed again after the decomposition of the flesh and red-ochre solution was applied to the bones. Undisturbed condition of the parts suggest that the bones were not lifted but red-ochre solution was sprinkled in large quantity.

Two pieces of animal bones (extremeties of long bones) are also lying near the pelvis along with one soap-stone circular disc, with three perforations in a straight line.

Skull:- (Pl. XA) Skull is resting on its right side facing towards west. Only the left norma-lateralis portion is visible in in-situ condition. Due to the pressure and the ashy deposit of the pit, skull is badly crushed and has cracked from numerous places. Almost all the sutures are wide open and none show any sign of advanced ossification.

Skull has been painted with red-ochre and on the vault eleven circular holes have been cut (trepanned) before it was burried. In norma lateralis position, on the left parietal bone between bregma and lambda there are seven finished and four unfinished holes. It seems that the holes might have been made with some sharp circular instrument (bone or stone) when the bone was still fresh. The holes are perfectly circular and all are of the same diameter (0.062m). (Pl. XII)

De-Morgan States in 'Prehistoric Man'[1] that the neolithic people cut circular portions from the skulls, trepanned them, not with any surgical end in view as in this operation today, but in order to obtain 'fetishes', for these circular pieces were pierced with holes that they might be suspended or worn as part of a necklance. The Gauls also indulged in this practice. In the oppidum of stradonitz in Bohemia, a fragment of a brain case, decorated with engraved geometric designs, has been discovered, this is evidence of a custom that exists to this day in Oceania'.

Occipital bone is partly visible and has broken into at least four major pieces on the left side. Lambda is intact. Left lambdoid and coronal sutures are intact. One circular sutural bone is present between the sphenoid angle of the parietal bone and the greater wing of the sphenoid.

Left parietal bone has cracked into three major pieces One crack is running right from the sagittal to the temporal suture. Greater wing of left sphenoid is totally missing and a hole has been pierced just near the pterion point. Fortunately the left temporal bone is more of less intact along with the zygomatic process. Mastoid

1. De Morgan. *Prehistoric Man.*

process, mastoid portion and parietal notch, all are intact. Mastoid process is prominent but not much pronounced. Porion point, mandibular fossa and suprameatal trangle, are intact. Left zygomatic bone is in articulated condition.

Frontal bone is broken just from the centre and gives the false impression of sagittal suture extending further to the glabella point. Left half of the frontal bone is visible and has collapsed. It has broken along the supraciliary arch. Left supra orbital notch and maxilla are intact. Frontal process of maxilla, left nasal bone and nasal spine are present. Left eye-orbit is present but due to the displacement of maxilla downwards, it is incomplete. All the teeth of the left side are present with only the 3rd molar disturbed from its socket. Cusps of the teeth are not worn out to any remarkable degree.

Only the left mandible is visible which is represented by small fragments. It is completely pressed and hardly anything worth study, can be lifted. Second and third molar, two premolars, canine and two incissors of the left side are visible. Cusps are not worn out.

All the skull bones are extremely fragile. Mastoid process is not markedly prominent, upper margin of the eye orbit is sharp.

Only a fragment of left-clavicle is present. Left scapula has broken into several pieces and has more or less completely disintegrated. Dorsal aspect of it is visible. Borders and the inferior angle, is completely missing. Glenoid cavity is partly present in the form of an impression on the earth. Acromion and the spine are present while the coracoid process is missing.

Right scapula is in badly damaged condition and a portion of the lateral border and plate, is visible.

Vertebral column has disintegrated into powdery mass and hardly any thing can be lifted. The column is in curved condition due to the crouching position of the skeleton. Only one or two ribs of the left side have escaped disintegration while the rest have completely disintegrated.

Humerus:- Left humerus is more or less intact except that it has broken into two pieces. It is in articulated condition and is running over the mandible. Its posterior aspect is visible. Head is near the glenoid cavity. Greater tubercle is not visible while the anatomical neck, shaft, lateral and medical supracondylar ridges, olecranon fossa, lateral and medical epicondyles and trochlea, all are in good condition.

Only the lower end of the right humerus is visible as it is running just below the left humerus. Here also the coracoid fossa, capitulum, radial fossa and epicondyles are intact.

Radius and Ulna:- Hands have been kept in folded condition. Left forearm is running over the lower end of right humerus. Left hand is bent upwards to its fullest extent. Lower ends of left radius and ulna are missing, while the shaft has broken into three major pieces. Upper ends are hidden by the lower end of left humerus. Right forearm is bent at an angle of nearly 90 degrees. Head and neck of right radius are intact and so also the olecranon process and trochlear notch.

Bones from both the hands are missing.

Pelvis: Only a mass of fragments and an impression on the earth is left to remind of the pelvic-girdle. Fragments left are extremely fragile and is practically impossible to lift anything worth studying.

Femur: Legs have been bent to a considerable extent. Left femur is in several pieces. At the upper end head, neck and lesser trochanter regions have broken into several pieces. Shaft has also broken at the lower end.

Anterior aspect of left femur is visible. Medial and lateral condyle and epicondyles are broken. Patellar surface is intact.

Right femur is lying in its position. It has also broken into several pieces at the upper end but the head seems to be intact. Medial condyle and epicondyle along with the patellar surface are intact.

Tibia and Fibula: Left tibia is lying close to the left femur and is in extremely damaged condition. Upper end is partly present while the distal end has completely disintegrated.

Left fibula is completely missing except for one or two small fragments adhering to the shaft of left tibia.

Right leg is lying below the left thigh and leg. A part of upper end of tibia is visible which is in total disintegrated condition.

Patella of both the sides are present in articulated condition, clinging to the patellar surface of their respective femur. Their apex and facets are intact.

Foot Bones: Foot bones are in extremely fragile condition. They are in more or less articulated condition. None of the tarsal bones are complete. Except for two metatarsal bones, others are complete and in somewhat better condition. Some of the phalanges are lying scattered.

MEASUREMENTS

Length of left humerus	=	29.5 cms
Length of femur (Right)	=	43.0 cms
Length of femur (left)	=	43.0 cms

Length of the skeleton from skull vault to the foot (Left) = 89 cms.

The skeleton belongs to that of a female aged between 25 to 30 years.

SKELETON NO. 8 (Pl. XI)

A human burial is found in the grave pit in the area BZH-1. The grave pit is more ore less circular and has been cut in layer 9 (disintegrated mud structure), sealed by pit-3. Top of the pit is at the depth of 2.80m from the present surface level and the skeleton is lying at the depth of 3.10m B.S. Approximate diameter of the grave pit is 1.20m.

The skeleton is lying in crouching position in the south-east, north-west direction. Skull is towards south-east while the feet towards north-west. Phalanges of the hand are touching the south-eastern edge while phalanges of the right leg are touching the north-western edge of the grave pit.

Maximum length of the skeleton in in-situ condition is 1.20m Filling of the pit consists of disintegrated mud and yellowish floor material. Its inner side has not been plastered by *"Chunam."* The pit is egg-shaped in section, wider towards bottom and narrower towards the top.

The skeleton is lying on its left side and almost all the parts are in articulated condition. Five carnelian barrel beads are found in the neck portion of the skeleton. All the beads are of different sizes. Probably these beads formed a necklace which was being worn by the deceased at the time of her death.

Skull:- (Pls. XII A & B) The skull is lying in its noma-lateralis position, resting on its left side.

Unfortunately the facial bones and the mandible are badly damaged. None of the sutures show any sign of fusion. Skull vault is curved and forehead is prominent. Occipital, temporal, parietal and frontal bones are more or less intact with several cracks particularly in the frontal bone. External occipital protuberance is intact. Foramen magnum is hidden. Vault is safe. Mastoid portion of right temporal and right styloid process are missing, while the right mastoid process and external acoustic meatus are intact. Right zygomatic bone is present but the zygomatic arch is missing except for a portion of zygomatic process upto the aricular tubercle. Greater wing of right sphenoid is missing. All the bones inside the right orbit are absent. Right supra orbital foramen is present. Nasal bone and frontal process of right maxilla are present. Maxilla below the region of nasal bone is completely broken and except for the portion containing teeth, other portions are missing. Anterior nasal spine is abscent. Two incisors, canine, two premolars and one molar of the right side of the maxilla are intact.

Only the right half of mandible is visible and has broken near the mental tubercle. Mental foramen is intact. Only three molars are present while the other teeth are displaced from their sockets and are not visible.

All the parts of the skull are extremely fragile. Upper edge of the orbits are quite sharp and facial bones are smoother.

Vertebral column is in curved state due to the crouching position of the body. Most of the vertebrae are hidden by scapula. 4th and 5th lumber vertebrae and sacrum, are visible and are in articulation with the hip bone. Lateral part of the right side of sacrum is slightly damaged. Tubercles are in fairly good condition. First segment of coccyx is also present.

Sternum:- Sternum is present and is slightly displaced from its proper position. It is extremely fragile. The manubrium is intact with its notches. Body of the sternum is broken on the left edge below the notch for the 4th costal cartilage. On the right side all the notches are complete. Xiphoid process is missing. Second, third, fourth and fifth segments of the sternum have united and first and second have also come very near to union.

Clavicle:- Only the sternal ends of both the clavicles are visible and are lying close to each other. Both are in good condition. Acromial ends are hidden by the head of the right humerus.

Scapula:- Right scapula is visible and is in articulated condition. It has broken into several pieces and is extremely fragile. Glenoid cavity is intact but the lateral borders, scapular plate and the inferior angle are damaged. Spine is broken and thus the acromion process has separated from the body of the scapula. Coracoid process is not visible but the superior angle is intact.

Ribs:- First rib of right side is broken but the tubercle is safe. Nearly all the twelve ribs are present but in damaged and extremely fragile condition. Their heads are not visible. Ribs from the left side are only partly visible.

Humerus:- Hands are folded upwards. Both the humerii are in articulation and in good condition. Head of the left humerus is not visible as it is obstructed by the scapula. Except for a slight damage at the medial condyle of left humerus, shafts and lower ends of both the humerii are in good state of preservation. Head, anatomical neck, surgical neck, greater and lesser tubercles of right humerus are safe. Capitulum, trochlea, coronoid fossa and lateral epicondyles of both the humerii are intact.

Radius and Ulna:- A part of the lower thirds of the left radius and ulna is hidden as the right humerus is passing over it. Both the fore-arms are folded in such way that the two palms are close to each other. Shafts, upper and lower ends of both the fore-arm bones are intact except for a crack at the neck of the right radius. Olecranon process, trochlear notch, coronoid process and head of both the ulnare are in good condition. Head, shaft, radial tuberosity and styloid process of the radii are in good condition.

Carpus and metacarpus:- Almost all the hand bones are present. Right hand bones are in proper position while the left hand bones are lying disturbed by the side of the lower end of the right radius.

Pelvis:- Because of the crouching position of the skeleton only the right half of the pelvis is visible. Pelvis is in articulated condition. External surface of right ilium and ischium are visible. Iliac crest along with the anterior inferior spine is quite intact. The surface has developed a long crack originating from the anterior-superior spine and running through the centre of the two thirds of the surface of ilium. Latissimus dorsi, posterior superior spine and posterior inferior spine, all are in fairly good condition. Ilium and ischium have been separated due to a wide crack at the point of their junction. Greater sciatic notch is intact and so also the auricular surface.

Only the ischium and iliac half of acetabular cavity is visible due to the presence of head of right femur. Spine of ischium, lesser ischiatic notch and tuberosity of right ischium are intact. The posterior border is complete.

Bones of the pelvis seem to be of delicate nature. Iliac fossa is shallower and the curves of the crest are not much pronounced. Upper part of the sacrum is straight.

Femur:- Both the femurii are folded nearly at right angles to the vertebral column.

Upper end of left femur is not visible while the remaining part is in good state of preservation. Shaft is intact. Popliteal surface, medial and lateral condyles are undamaged.

Anterior aspects of right femur is visible and is in good condition. Head, greater and lesser trochanter, inter-trochanteric line, shaft, medial and epicondyles, all are intact.

Both the patella are lying more or less in their respective positions. Apex and facets are intact.

Tibia:- Legs have been folded and kept in such a fashion that the right femur passes over the left leg and left feet bones are hidden by the lower end of the right tibia and fibula. Whole of left tibia is intact. Medial condyle, tubercles, shaft and medial malleous are in good condition. Similarly all the parts of right tibia are intact except for a slight damage of the medial condyle and a crack at the middle of the shaft.

Fibula:- Both the fibulae are in good condition. Lower end of left fibula is only slightly visible. Right fibula is riding over the lateral border of the right tibia and has also developed a wide crack at the middle of its shaft. Head, shaft, and lateral malleous, all are intact except the cracks referred to above.

Foot bones:- Tarsal and metatarsal bones of both the feet are intact and in articulated condition. Calcaneus, talus, cuboids, cuneiform, all are intact. Phalanges of the right feet are just touching the border of the pit.

The skeleton belongs to that of an adult female aged between 30 to 35 years.

MEASUREMENTS

Maximum length of right humerus	=	29.5 cms.
Maximum length of ulna (left)	=	25.0 cms.
Maximum length of ulna (right)	=	25.0 cms.
Maximum length of radius (right)	=	23.2 cms.
Maximum length of femur (right)	=	42.9 cms.
Maximum length of tibia (right)	=	35.2 cms.
Maximum length of fibula (right)	=	34.3 cms.
Maximum length of Calcaneus (right)	=	07.0 cms.

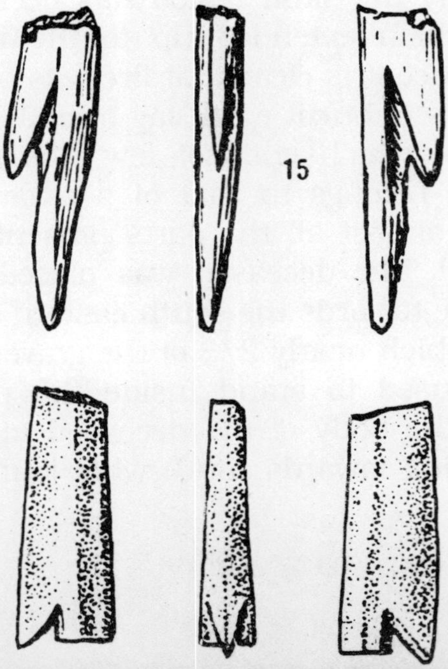

15

SKELETON NO. 9 (Pl. XIII)

A complete extended human burial is found in quadrant BZH-3(64), western extension of A1-A2. The circular grave pit is located inside the huge dwelling pit on the northern side. Diameter of the grave pit is roughly 0.975m to 1.0m. The pit is dome shaped, widest at the bottom and narrowest at the top. It has been cut in the filling of the dwelling pit which consists of yellowish earth (floor material) mixed with few stone pieces. Working level of the grave pit lies in layer 6. Central portion of the top of the grave pit has been disturbed by pits 2b and 2. Pit 2 is sealed by layer 4.

Maximum depth of the grave pit at the centre is 1.075m and maximum length in the section is 1.825m. A portion of the pit still remains in the section looking west, after the complete exposure of the skeleton. On the northern side the pit line joins the original pit line of the dwelling pit.

Filling of the grave pit consists of loose earth mixed with considerable amount of ash, stone pieces, several chunks of charcoal and redish burnt earth. It contains quite a good number of pot sherds. Charcoal from the grave pit has been collected for C-14 test.

Unfortunately the skull region has been badly damaged by the later pit 2b which extended up to the top of the skull region. From the evidence it is clear that fire was being burnt in pit 2b and thus big chunks of burnt earth lay over the skull and chest region, as a result of which ends of few ribs are found charred. The skeleton which belongs to that of a male is found in articulated condition with almost all the parts present. It is a fine case of an extended burial. The deceased was placed slightly away form the centre and more towards the south eastern side of the grave pit, and as a result of which nearly 2/3 of the grave pit is lying empty which was probably used to stand inside the pit by the persons who lowered down the body of the deceased inside the pit. They must have been looking towards south while putting the body inside the pit.

The Skeleton is lying at the depth of 2.975m below the present surface in supine position, oriented south-west to north-east. Skull is towards south-west with eyes looking east and the legs are towards north-east. Skull is slightly tilted towards right. Complete body, except for the hands, is in stretched condition. Right hand is bent at the ankle region, away from the pelvis, making an angle of nearly 110°-115° with the humerus. Fingers are folded towards the palm. Left hand is bent at the ankle region, making an angle of nearly 30° with humerus, so that the hand is lying stretched over the chest region just below the neck.

On the right of the skull just touching the right orbit and above the right parietal bone two stone pieces are lying. Another stone piece is lying near the right half of the mandible.

On the right of the right humerus away from its deltoid region a portion of stem of a hand made earthern stand is lying near the corner of the pit.

Skull:- The skull along with the mandible is lying in badly damaged condition. The damage has been caused by the people who dug pit 2b. Probably the diggers of pit 2b came across the skull and major portion of the left side of the skull got damaged. The stone by which the damage might have been caused can be seen thrusted inside the skull at the junction of left occipital, temporal and parietal bones.

The skull is tilted towards right so that its left lateral aspect is visible. Frontal bone has broken into several pieces. A wide crack has developed from the nasion point. Facial parts are heavily damaged. From the point of bregma to fronto-zygomatic suture and to asterian and inion point along with left mastoid process, zygomatic process is totally missing. Except for the left mastoid process which sunk inside the brain cavity, all other bones form the region mentioned above are missing.

Fortunately left eye orbit is complete though here also zygomatic bone and process have separated from each other.

Occipital bone is present in fairly good condition and so also the right temporal squamosal and parietal bones and mastoid process. Major portion of the nasal bone is present in small fragments. Anterior nasal spine is totally missing. Major portion of left maxilla is missing. Right maxilla is present in dislodged condition with heavy damages.

None of the sutures on left side are visible. Left infra-orbital foramen is present. All the teeth from the upper Jaw are missing.

Mandible is in extremely fragile and damaged state. Right ramus is not visible. Rest of the mandible has broken into three major pieces. Left ramus has separated from the point of angle. Body of the mandible has broken into two at the point of mental protuberance. Left ramus is badly damaged from the point of mandibular foramen along with the posterior border upto the angle. Left coronoid and condylar process of mandible are intact. Head of left mandible is also safe. Five teeth (2 molars, 2 premolars & one canine) of the right lower jaw are visible while only one premolar from left side is present. A canine is lying just above the right canine.

The skull is quite big in size and seems to be more in length then in breadth. Walls of the skull are quite thick. Glabella is prominent. Upper margin of the orbit is thick, rounded and rough. Forehead is slopy.

Vertebral Column:- Verterbral column is in good articulated condition and all the vertebrae from axis to coccyx are present. Cervical vertebra and thoracic upto 10th are hidden by the left hand and sternum respectively. 11th and 12th thoracic vertebrae are intact along with their spines. Lumbar vertebrae are in good condition.

Sacrum:- Pelvic surface of sacrum is visible and is in articulated condition. Four pairs of pelvic sacral foramina, transverse ridges, iliacus are intact. On the left side, upper surface of lateral part above first pelvic sacral foramen is damaged. Coccyx consisting of three rudimentary vertebrae fused together; is present in articulated condition.

Sternum:- Posterior aspect of sternum is visible. Manubrium is slightly dislodged from its position. Body of the sternum is extremely fragile and is damaged at the ridges.

Xiphoid process is missing. Notches for costal cartilage on the left border are present.

Ribs:- Almost all the ribs are present in extremely fragile condition.

Scapula:- Acromin and coracoid process, and a portion of glenoid cavity of left scapula are exposed. Of the right scapula, intact glenoid cavity, damaged coracoid process, acromion process and major portion of the body are visible.

Left clavicle is hidden while sternal end and body of the right clavicle are exposed.

Fore Limbs:- Right fore limb is bent at the ankle so that the hand has been placed over the chest or say over the cervicle and upper thoracic vertebrae. All the bones are in good and articulated condition. Left fore limb is also bent at the ankle in such a way that the fore arm is placed away from the hip bone.

Left hand bones are in full extended condition. Right hand is lying in supine position with the phalanges folded towards the wrist. Left humerus is in good articulated condition except for it has broken into two pieces, at the point of deltoid tuberosity. Lateral aspect of humerus is visible. Head, greater tubercle, anatomical neck, medial supra condylar ridge and medial epicondyle all are infact. Right humerus is lying in verticle position. It has cracked at several places and is very fragile. Head is intact with one crack but the portion between head and lesser tubercle is damaged. Cracks have developed at the upper and lower thirds of the shaft. All other points are intact. Head of both the humerii are lodged in their respective glenoid cavities.

Fore-Arm:- Left and right radius are in fairly good condition Head neck and styloid process are intact. Left ulna has broken to three pieces at the shaft region. Right ulna is complete.

Hand Bones:- All the bones of the left hand are present in good articulated condition except the fifth metacarpal bone which is damaged along with its phalanges. In right hand, trapezius and one or two phalanges are damaged.

Hip Bone:- Frontal view of hip bone is visible. Right half is much damaged in comparison to the left half. Left iliac bone is intact and in good condition. Anterior and posterior superior and inferior spines are intact. Crest of left ilium is intact. Acetabulum is present. Pubic crest is missing. Tuberosity of ischium is present. Pubic bone on both the sides are heavily damaged. Right iliac crest is intact. Posterior superior and inferior spines and anterior inferior spine, are present. Anterior superior spine is broken. Iliac surface has cracked into numerous small pieces. Acetabulum, except at the pubic region, is present. Ischiatic tuberosity is present but pubic tubercle is totally missing. Sacrum is big & curved. Depth of pubic symphysis is considerable and the distance between pubic tubercles is not much. Both the legs have been placed in supine position.

Femur: Both the femurii are long, strong and in articulated condition. Heads of both are lodge in their respective acetabular cavities. Head, greater and lesser trochanters, neck and intertrochanteric line of both are intact. Shafts are in good condition. Patellar surface, medial condyles and epicondyles of left femur are intact. Left femur is slightly damaged just above the lateral condyle. Lateral and epicondyle of right femur are intact whereas medial condyle is slightly damaged.

Patella: Left patella is missing while right is slightly disturbed from its position. It has broken into three pieces. Apex is intact.

Leg Bones: Right and left tibia are intact and in good condition. Left tibia is in two pieces. Medial condyle of left is intact while that of right is damaged, lateral condyles and tuberosities are in good condition. Surface and borders are intact. Both the fibulae are hidden below their respective tibia.

Foot Bones: Both the feet are lying in stretched supine position. Tarsus and metatarsus bones are present in articulated condition. Phalanges of both the first metatarsal bones (toe) are missing while the rest are present.

The skeleton belongs to that of male aged between 50 to 55 years.

D. MORPHOLOGICAL STUDIES[1]

i) Age	*about 5 yrs.*	*11-15 yrs.*	*26-30 yrs.*	*31-35 yrs.*	*46-50 yrs.*	*51-55 yrs.*
Skeleton No.	Skl.2	Skl.4	Skl.7	Skl.3	Skl.1	Skl.5
						Skl.6
			Skl.10	Skl.8		Skl.9

ii) Sex	*Male*	*Female*
	Skl.1, Skl.5, Skl.6, Skl.9, Skl.10	Skl.3, Skl.7, Skl.8

Sex of the child (Skl. No. 2) and that of the juvenile (Skl. No. 4) could not be determined as in the crania of such children sex is almost difficult to determine due to non development of characteristic features.

1. Basu Arbinda and Anadi Pal, *Human Remains from Burzahom*, Calcutta, 1980.

iii) Craniometry

	Male		*Female*		*Child*
	Skl.1	*Skl.6*	*Skl.7*	*Skl.8*	*Skl.2*
Max. cranial length	190.00	187.0	185.0	190.0	162.0
Max. cranial breadth	133.00	140.0	127.0	129.0	118.0
Nasion-inian length	176.0	174.0	—	178.0	138.0
Length-breadth index	70.0	74.9	68.7	67.9	72.8
Length-height index	73.7	—	—	—	74.1
Breadth-height index	105.3	—	—	—	101.7
Length-auricular height index	66.3	63.6	64.3	63.2	—
Breadth-auricular height index	94.7	85.0	93.7	93.0	—
Transverse-fronto-parietal index	73.7	69.3	69.3	75.2	66.1

iv) Cranial Capacity in C.C.

Male		*Female*	
Skl.1	*Skl.6*	*Skl.7*	*Skl.8*
1493.16	1469.01	1352.90	1413.34

The values obtained fall into aristencephalic class indicating high cranial capacity for the Burzahom skulls.

The neurocranial measurements of maximum cranial length and breadth show that Burzahom skulls are dolichocranic (L-B index in three out of four skulls: 68.7 - 70.0). Male skull no 6 is having cranial index value of 74.9 and lies in the border of dolicho and mesocranic category. This skull is characterised by high values of cranial breadth (140 mm.) bi-auricular breadth (133 mm), bi-orbital breadth (116 mm.), bi-molar breadth (116 m.m.), bi-zygomatic breadth (150 mm), maxillo alveolar breadth (71 mm) and nasal breadth (33 m.m.)

The male skull No. 1 and two female skulls (Skl. 7 & 8) have much similarity on the cranio-facial dimensions and proportions. They are markedly orthognathus as evident from facial profile angle, which ranges between 87° to 90°. In cranial index these skulls are dolichrocranic.

The three skulls (Skl.1. 8 & 7) represent precisely the same population.

Basic Burzahom skulls are closer to mature Harappan skulls from cemetery R. 37.

v) Cranioscopic Observations

	Male		Female	
	Skl.1	*Skl.6*	*Skl.8*	*Skl.7*
Cranial contour	ovoid	broad ovoid	long ovoid	long ovoid
Forehead slope	receding	highly receding	slightly receding	slightly receding
Nasal profile	concave	—	straight	—
Shape of nasal bones	narrow constricted	—	narrow constricted	— —
Facial prognathism	Orthognathous	Orthognathus	Orthognathous	Orthognathous

In cranioscopic observations also male skull No. 6 is distinctly different from the remaining three crania. The major differences seem to be primarily due to robusticity and gross size. Skl. no 6 is appreciably broader in cerebral and facial region. It is distinguished by very low and highly receding forehead, markedly retreating frontal bone with no frontal eminences, low arched vertex, rounded occipit, wide ovoid cranial contour due to swollen parietals, very wide and prominent molar bones, low rectangular orbit, wide nasal aperture and very wide palate.

Remaining three skulls (male skull No. 1, female skull nos. 7 & 8) however, resemble mutually in cranioscopic observations and are morphologically fairly similar. Cranial contour in male is ovoid in shape and in females long ovoid. This is because occipital protuberance is less pronounced in males and more pronounced in females.

vi) Dentition

Dental Caries : Out of 78 molars examined, teeth with carious infection is only in two upper molars of which one is on the first and the other on the third molar. The other teeth are unaffected. Out of 59 pre-molars the ante-mortem tooth loss is observed only in one right second premolar of mandible. Only two maxillae [Skl. 3 & 6 (Pl. XIVA)] show the pulp exposure on their first molars. The alveolar bone destruction of medium category is found in the left first maxillary molar of skl. no. 1. The tendency of tartar deposition is almost equal in both the jaws, where medium degree of deposition is abscent. The dental health condition was sound, though general wear and tear was marked to an extreme degree of attrition. This was probably due to mixing of siliceous material in the food as was also found at Kalibangan. Mandible of Skl. No. 8 shows dental abscess cavity (Pl. XIVB).

vii) The Postcranial bones: In general, extremity bones of Burzahom skeletons are long and powerful in structure, however male Skl. No. 6 is an exception, having much shorter but sturdier bones compared to other male individuals. Much robustness of the limb bones of the specimen No. 6 is clearly visible.

The perforation of fossa olecrani (septal aperture) is seen in one humerus only (left of Skl. No. 1) A platymeric protrusion is present in both right and left femur of skeleton No. 9. It consists of a lateral flange or bulge at the lateral margin of the subtrochanteric flattening. A typical 'squatting facet' is observed on right and left tibiae of skeleton No. 9 and right tibia of skeleton No. 1. This tibio-calcaneal facet infer postural differences associated with habitual position.

MEASUREMENTS OF LONG BONES - MAXIMUM LENGTH

MALE

	Skl.1		*Skl.6*	*Skl.9*		*Skl.10*	*Mean*		
	Rt.	*Lt.*	*Lt.*	*Rt.*	*Lt.*	*Rt.*	*Rt.*	*Lt.*	*Rt.+Lt.*
Humerus	338.0	338.0	324.0	337.0	337.0	328.00	334.0	333.0	333.7

FEMALE

Skl.8	
Rt.	Lt.
300.0	295.0

MALE

	Skl.1		*Skl.6*	*Skl.9*		*Skl.10*	*Mean*		
	Rt.	*Lt.*	*Lt.*	*Rt.*	*Lt.*	*Rt.*	*Rt.*	*Lt.*	*Rt.+Lt.*
Radius	258.0	257.0	251.0	267.0	264.0	270.0	265.0	257.3	261.2

FEMALE

Skl.8	*SKl. No. 3*		*Mean*	
Rt.	*Rt.*	*Lt.*	*Rt.*	*Rt.+Lt.*
225.0	225.00	228.0	228.5	228.3

MALE

	Skl.1		*Skl.6*	*Skl.9*		*Skl.10*	*Mean*		
	Rt.	*Lt.*	*Rt.*	*Rt.*	*Lt.*	*Rt.*	*Rt.*	*Lt.*	*Rt.+Lt.*
Ulna	282.0	283.0	273.0	289.0	288.0	294.0	284.5	285.5	284.8

FEMALE

Skl.3	*SKl. No. 8*		*Mean*	
Rt.	*Rt.*	*Lt.*	*Rt.*	*Rt.+Lt.*
244.0	254.00	248.0	249.5	248.7

MALE

	Skl.1		*Skl.6*	*Skl.9*		*Skl.10*		*Mean*	
	Rt.	*Lt.*	*Rt.*	*Rt.*	*Lt.*	*Rt.*	*Lt.*	*Rt.*	*Lt.*
Femur Absolute length	464.0	*467.0*	450.0	472.0	473.0	458.0	460.0	461.0	466.7
								Rt. + Lt.	
								463.4	
Length in natural position	458.0	463.0	—	467.0	467.0	455.0	455.0	460.0	461.7
								Rt. + Lt.	
								460.8	
Robusticity Index	12.7	11.9	—	11.7	12.3	12.5	11.8	12.3	12.0
								Rt. + Lt.	
								12.2	

FEMALE

	Skl. 3	*Skl. 8*			*Mean*
	Lt.	*Rt.*	*Lt.*	*Lt.*	*Rt. + Lt.*
Absolute length	393.0	463.0	437.0	415.0	422.0
Length in natural position	—	431.5	433.0	—	432.3
Robusticity index	—	12.3	12.4	12.4	12.4

MALE

	Skl. 1		*Skl. 6*		*Skl. 9*		*Skl. 10*	*Mean*	
	Rt.	*Lt.*	*Rt.*	*Lt.*	*Rt.*	*Lt.*	*Lt.*	*Rt.*	*Lt.*
Tibia Maximum length	386.0	392.0	371.0	373.0	409.0	409.0	408.0	388.7	395.5
								Rt. + Lt.	
								393.0	

FEMALE

	Skl. 8 Rt.	Skl. 8 Lt.	Mean Rt. + Lt.
Maximum length	357.0	354.0	355.5
Rolusticity index	19.6	19.8	19.7

ESTIMATED STATURE - MALE

	Skl. 1	Skl. 6	Skl. 9	Skl. 10	Mean
Average (Rt.+Lt.)	1756.0	1719.1	1779.0	1760.0	1753.5

FEMALE

	Skl. 3	Skl. 8	Mean
as per Troiter and Gleser Interracial formulae	1528.6	1570.3	1549.5

MALE

Pearsons Regression formulae	1696.2	1665.4	1717.3	1704.0	1695.7

FEMALE

	1563.9	1633.6	1598.8

MALE

General Formulae Dupertuis and Hadden	1764.5	1734.9	1785.5	1771.3	1764.1

FEMALE

	1590.9	1637.6	1614.3

For both males and females the length of the arms is nearly 70 percent of that of the leg. The intermembral index thus indicates that Burzahom people possessed relatively long legs in relation to arms as is the case with the present day population of the valley.

E. DISCUSSION

The results of cranioscopic observations indicate that at Burzahom during Neolithic period long headed dolichoranic individuals were the basic population. The major features were: long narrow head, protruding occiput, some what low receding forehead, medium to prominent supraorbital ridges, prominent glabella, high vertical porion height, and sturdy built with tall to medium stature. There is no evidence of brachycranic skull in either sex.

Skull No. 6 has greater cranial width, markedly wider bizygomatic and bimastoid breadth, very wide nasal breadth, and low nasal height. On the basis of this bone variant it is not possible to state whether it is an expected variant or it represents a different population group. The racial features clearly indicate that, as stated by the author earlier, there was no racial connection whatsoever of neolithic people of Burzahom or for that matter Kashmir with those of the north-west and south China as earlier postulated by the excavator and some other scholars.

The racial characters clearly pointout their association towards southern Russian and west Asia. On the basis of antiquities and domestication of plants as per evidence from Gufkral, this presumption was further strengthened. It can not be denied that during neolithic period there were trade connections both with south China, South Russia and West Asia. Rather Kashmir was on the trade route between the two remote areas.

The similarity of racial features of Burzahom skeletons with those of the present day population of plains of Jammu, Punjab and Haryana and with those of the cemetery R. 37 of mature Harappa culture most probably reflects their genetic affinity, and probably also hints towards an ethnic continuity. The presence of carnelian beads both at Burzahom and at Gufkral in the neolithic levels and a typical Harappan pot at Burzahom point out towards contact between the two people, though meagre, and culturally far apart. The carbon 14 dates for neolithic period of Burzahom and Gufkral (2500-1500 B.C.) and those of the Harappan culture show that as both the cultures were existing side by side there is bound to be some contact between the two.

It will not be out of place to mention the racial features of skeletal remains of some of the neolithic sites of India to demonstrate the racial horizon that existed during the same cultural period in different zones. Neolithic people of Brahmagiri (Karnataka) were mesobrachycephalic, medium stature, robust in constitution with broad nose. Sarkar[1] has found them to be of Scytho-Iranian stock and to an autochthonous race of proto-Australoid. Neolithic people of Piklihal (A.P.) were of robust construction, with large head and tall stature. They could be the ancestors of a major element of the present mixed so-called Dravidian speaking people of Deccan and Southern India. Maski in Karnataka has yielded three physical types- i) Mesobrachy cranic type (Scytho-Iranian); ii) long headed, large brained and stoutly built; iii) long headed, broad based similar to autochthonous Australian type. The neolithic cattle keepers of TekkalKota (A.P.) were of medium to tall stature, long headed with large cranial capacity and variable nose form. They were of sturdy built. Neolithic skulls from NagarjunaKonda (A.P.) were long headed.

At present the major portion of India seems to be inhabited by a medium statured, mesocephalic and dolichocephalic, mesorrhine population. The population tends to have more dolichocephals in peninsular India, while occassionally there is also some amount of brachycephaly, as in the extreme south. All over India, there are now areas of short to medium stature, dolichocephalic, mesorrhine and chemarrhine population, known as proto-Australoid (Guha)[2] or Veddoid. Opinion has been expressed that this population covered the entire Northern Indian plains at one time. The north-western

1. Sarkar S.S. 'Human skeletal remains from Brahmnagiri. *Bulletin of Deptt. of Anthropology*, 9(i), Calcutta, 1960.
2. Guha, B.S. 'Racial Affinities of the People of India: *Census* - 1931, Simla, 1935.

portion of the northern plains has a tall dolichocephalic, leptorrhine population. The powerfully built, large brained race with well developed supra-orbital regions and enormous growth of the post-auricular parts of skull, identified from various Harappan sites, survives to this day in the population of north-western part of the Indian sub-continent. The more dedicately made smaller type with sharp well cut features, fine narrow nose from Indus valley, which is close to mediterranean race, has entered largely the composition of the population of North especially in the upper strata of the society. The population of Indus valley and Kashmir Valley appears to have remained more or less stable in character from Harappan times and neolithic times, respectively to the present day.

Evidence of trephinatian in the hyperdolichocranic female skull (Skl. No. 7) from neolithic levels at Burzahom points out to vary ancient custom. Incidentally this skull was painted with red-ochre solution. In norma lateralis position, on the left parietal bone between bregma and lambda seven finished circular holes with diameters varying from 8 mm. to 13 mm. and four unfinished circular depressions ranging in diameters between 7 mm. to 10 mm. were noticed. From the nature of the cutting none of the perforations seem to be of *ante-mortem* origin. These trephinations appear to have been made with some sharp instrument with circular cutting edges (bone or stone), when the bone was green as the margins of the perforations do not show any osteogenesis in the form of callous formation. The exposed diploic spaces of spongy inner table show no signs of closing. The cutting edges of the circular openings are neither smooth nor bevelled indicating that these perforations were made post-mortem. As the perforations were made post-mortem, when the bone was still green, they were certainly not for the sake of any surgical operation but appear to be connected with some sort of magico-religious belief. Probably they were made to obtain roundels for use as amulets. These holes were made when the skeleton was re-exposed after the decomposition of the flesh, to be treated with red-ochre solution. De-Morgan[1] has mentioned that "the neolithic people cut circular portions from

1. De-Morgan, *'Prehistoric Man'*. London, 1984.

skulls-trephanned them, not with any surgical end in view as is in this operation to-day, but in order to obtain 'fetishes' for these circular pieces were pierced with holes that they might be suspended or worn as part of a necklace. The Gauls also indulged in this practice. In the oppidum of Stradonitz in Bohemia a fragment of a brain case, decorated with engraved geometric designs has been discovered; this is evidence of a custom that exists to this day in Oceania."

Gillman[1] has described a series of cases of cranial perforations from Michigan. These have always been regarded as post-mortem cuts made for the purpose of cranial amulets.

Cases of treating the skeleton with red-ochre solutions during prehistoric times are not lacking. Josef Augusta[2] mentions about the grave of a youngman in Grotte du Cavillian which was sprinkled with red ochre during late palaeolithic times.

A number of human skulls were found burried with ochre in Neolithic deposits of two pits cut in Azilian times in the cave burial at Ofnet in Bavaria. In the graves of Auragnacian mammoth hunters in middle of Brono, body was sprinkled with red ochre. In Vestonia, a female skeleton was put in crouching position and sprinkled with red-ochre.

For a modern ethnological parallel we can refer to the very similar practice among the 'palaeolithic' Onge pigmies of the Andaman Islands mentioned by Capriani.[3] The Onges bury their dead under the floor of the hut, each being buried under his own bed. Seven days after the burial they break off the jaw bone of the deceased, paint it with red ochre and decorate it, using it as an ornament or a necklace. About three months later they exhume all the bones, wash them, paint them with red ochre and bury them again in the same place.

---

1. Gillman, H. On the prehistoric trephining and cranial amulets. *North American Ethnology*, Washington, 1882.
2. Josef Augusta - *Prehistoric Man*, london, 1960.
3. Capriani, *Illustrated London News*, February 3, 1962.

5

ANIMAL BURIALS

A. NEOLITHIC AND MEGALITHIC PERIODS

In the history of mankind, the instinct of love and affection for the deceased perhaps took shape in the form of burials, more than fifty thousand years back.[1] It was the beginning of an instinct which later on culminated in making of such magnificent edifices as pyramids in Egypt and Taj in India.[2] In due course this instinct was not only confined to relatives but brought in its fold his pets too. From this, one may surmise a totemic value or a ritualistic significance to these practices.

At Le Moustier[3] in southern France, a Neanderthal youth was buried by his fellows in a shallow grave. With him charred animal bones and flint implements were also deposited. Near Machai in the mountains of Baysun-tau in Central Asia Neanderthal boy aged about nine years was buried in a grave, his head surrounded by horns of Siberian ibex (*Capra sibirica*). Ibex cult still exists in Central Asia. Neanderthal hunters of Drachenloch used to carry out

---

1. F. E. Zeuner, *Dating the past* (London, 1950), p.298, and Cesare Emiliani, Dating human evolution. *The evolution of man*, Vol. II (Chicago, 1960), p.64.
2. V. Gordon Childe, *Man Makes Himself* (London, 1937), p.62.
3. Josef Augusta, *Prehistoric Man* (London, 1960).

rites of a mysterious cult in their caves, after a successful hunt, and bury the bones and skulls of cave bears carefully in stone graves. At Alaca Huyuk[1] (2400-2200 B.C.) a king was buried by the side of his queen along with the body of his dog. On top of the timber roofing of the tomb, skulls of the slaughtered oxen were placed. At Dorak in Troy (2553-2559 B.C.) a dog was buried along with the king. The Nile Dwellers in the Nile valley forced the dog to accompany his master to the other world and buried with him in the tomb. In India, the practice of burying the animals and particularly the dogs in regular grave pits has been recorded in the excavations at Burzahom, Kashmir during 1962 and 1963[2]. From Nagarjunakonda excavations skeletal remains of a deer in association with two intact pots, were recovered from a neolithic pit.[3] This appears to be a case of intentional burial.

B. ANIMAL BURIAL TYPES

Most of the animal burials belong to Period III of occupation, while Period II (2375 ± 120 B.C.) is represented by one or two cases. Period I has so far not yielded any evidence of animal or human burials. From the available evidence it appears that the custom of burying their pet animals was of common occurrence in Period III than in Period II. In Period II it was just taking shape. The animals were buried in regular grave pits. The burial pits were oval in shape i.e., narrower towards the top and wider towards the bottom. They varied in diameter from 0.90 m. to 1.05 m. Only in one case form Period II, the pit was of irregular shape. In one case the pit was plastered with 'Chunam' from inside, as in case of most of the human burial pits. The pit filling generally consisted of ashy material mixed with clay and stone pieces. Three modes of burying the animals or their bones have been noticed. In all the cases except one, the body was placed inside the pit in north-south direction with the skull region towards north and caudal end towards south. In case of the exception the skeleton had east-west orientation. The animal burial types are described below.

---

1. Stuart Piggott, *The Dawn of Civilazation* (New York, 1961), pp. 165-168.
2. *Indian Archaeology* — 1962-63 — *A Review* (New Delhi, 1965), p. 9-10.
3. *Indian Archaeology* — 1959-60 — *A Review* (New Delhi, 1960), p. 6.

i) In the first type pet or other animals were sacrificed to honour the dead person and some bones of the animal were picked up probably after making a feast of the flesh of the sacrificed. These picked up bones were deposited along with the human body[1] in the same grave pit either at a higher or at the same level, where the human body was put. In one case, skull of a dog was deposited, whereas in other cases fragmentary bones of goat and antler were interned with the human skeleton. At times the animal bones were also treated with red ochre solution along with the human bones.

ii) The second type is fractional burial. This is represented by three examples, two from Period III and one from Period II. In the latter case (Pl. XV) in a large egg shaped pit having diameter of 1.35 m., fragmentary bones of wild dogs along with two antlers of Barasingha (*Cervus duvauceli*) were noticed. The dogs were represented by five intact skulls to which were attached portions of vertebral columns in articulated condition. Other fragmentary bones recovered from the pit were mostly ribs, limb bones and fragments of pelvic girdles. All the loose bones had fracture marks. From the condition of the bones it appears that the dogs (which incidentally all belonged to the wild variety) were sacrificed, stripped of their flesh and then ceremonially buried. Filling of the pit was devoid of any ashy material. Below the level of this assemblage nothing else was recovered from the pit. The pit was cut in the floor of a house.

In another fractional burial, disarticulated bone fragments belonging to that of a Himalayan Ibex (*Capra falconerid*, Pl. XVI) were deposited in the pit at a depth of 1.90 m. below the present surface in the same pit, whereas at a lower depth (2.20 m.) fragmentary bones of antler, dog, sheep and goat were deposited.

iii) In the third mode of disposal, the pet animals were deposited inside the burial pits either single (Pl. XVII) or in two, in the same pit at different levels. This type of burials were mostly of dogs and in two case of wolves (Pl. XVIII). In both the cases *i.e.*, single and double, the body of the animal was kept in north-south orientation,

1. A.K. Sharma, 'Neolithic human Burials from Burzahom', Kashmir, *Journal, Oriental Institute*. Vol. XVI, No. 3 (Baroda, 1967), pp. 240-242.

in crouching position i.e. sitting at ease either resting on its right side or left side. Only in one case the skeleton of a dog was found to be lying in supine position, resting on its back with legs upwards.

In almost all the cases of this type of disposal, bones were found in well preserved condition. The length of the skeletons in situ condition, from the skull to the caudal region varied from 0.60-0.86 m. In case of complete double burials both the skeletons deposited at different levels in the same pit were that of the dogs. Only in one case the one at a higher level was probably that of a wolf. Of the two single primary burials unearthed, one belonged that of a wolf while the other to that of a dog. In case of wolf bones, those in articulated condition were completely charred. The pit was filled with large quantity of ash. The articulated condition of this skeleton points out that firstly the dead body of the animal was put inside the pit and then limited inhumation was performed. The pit was later on filled up. The significance of this rather ritualistic operation is only a matter of conjecture.

Broad Inferences

In the sequel the following facts may be enumerated form the animal burials of Burzahom.

1. Like human beings, animals were also buried in regularly dug grave pits inside the habitation area itself.
2. Orientation of human and animal skeletons was generally common i.e. north-south, with skull facing east or west.
3. Pet animals like dog, stag, goat were sacrificed during the disposal of human body and some parts of one or more of these animals were deposited along with the human skeleton in the same pit.
4. Burial of two animals in the same pit was a common practice. From the location of these pits it appears that they were in continuous use by the members of the same family.
5. No antiquity has been reported from animal graves.

At present it appears that the neolithic people of Burzahom were exclusively practising the burials of the dead animals, since no evidence of this sort has been reported form eastern or southern neolithic sites in India except a probable case from Nagarjunkonda. This can be further confirmed if some more sites are excavated and reports are published.

Why of all the animals only dog, wolf and ibex were given such a systematic and special treatment? It appears that these animals had some totemic relationship with their masters.

It is interesting to note that in Burzahom during early neolithic period two types of domesticated dogs a) smaller but stouter like the mastiff and b) the taller one like the Greyhound were present. They continued during the Megalithic period also. It is well known fact on the basis of evidence from European sites that the dog was domesticated in Europe for hunting in post-glacial mesolithic times (8000 B.C.) and the domestic species, *Canis familiaris* Linn first appeared there during the Neolithic period.[1] In India we do get evidence of domesticated dogs. From Utnur[2] (2295 ± 155 B.C.), Tekkalkota[3] (1675 B.C.), Pikklihal[4] (2000 B.C.) bones of dogs have not been reported. Bones of dogs obtained form Mohenjo-daro (1650 B.C)[5], Harappa and Rupar excavation[6] have been identified as belonging to that of the domestic dogs, *Canis familiaris* Linn, having affinity with those of the near-east. The remains of *Canis familiaris* Linn have also been recorded from Sialk and Shah Tepe in Iran. Similarly the same has been observed at Kalibangan[7] (1960 B.C.),

1. Zittel, Karl A. Von, *Text Book of Palaeontology* (London, 1925), pp. 316.
2. F.R. Allchin, *Utnur Excavations* (Hyderabad, 1961), p. 62.
3. M.S. Nagaraja Rao & K.C. Malhotra, *The Stone-age hill dwellers of Tekkalkota*, (Poona, 1965), pp. 87.
4. F.R. Allchin, *Piklihal Excavations*, (Hyderabad, 1960), p. 119.
5. Edward S. Deevey, Richard Foster Flint, Irving Rouse, *Radiocarbon*, Vol.6, (Connecticut, 1966).
6. Op.cit.
7. Report of Zoological Survey of India.

Nevasa[1] (1250 ± 125 B.C.) and from sub period IB of Brahmagiri[2] (1000 B.C.). Dogs form Harappan sites strongly resemble the modern Indian Pariah, Dingo and Mastiff types. But none of the above mentioned sites have yielded the wild variety. It is in Phase II of Burzahom that we do get, wild variety also. From this evidence of wild and domesticated varieties occurring together should we infer that the domestication of dog took place in neolithic period independently, some time during C. 2500 B.C. in Kashmir region ? However, its erlier appearance is attested to in other regions in Harappa culture. According to Prasad and Nath[3] the Indian domesticated dogs descended from Canis tenggeranus kohbrugge of the Oriental region in the South-East-Asia in the Diluvial times and from it were derived the Pariah, the Greyhound and the Tibet dog.

At Burzahom from the neolithic period bones of dog (*Canis familiaris* Linn), Kashmir stag (*Cervus elaphus* hanglu Wagner), wild boar (*Sus scrofa* Linn), domestic pig (*Sus cristatus* Wagner), wolf (*Canis Lupas* Linn.), nilgai, (*Boselaphus trago camelus* Pallas), Gaur (*Bos garus* H. Smith), the domestic humped cattle (*Bos indicus* Linn), the Indian bison (*Bubalus bulalis* Linn.), wild urial (*Ovis orientalis* Vignei Blyth), the Argali (*Ovis ammon* Linn.), domestic goat (*Capra hircus* Linn) and domestic sheep (*Ovis orientalis* Gwelin) have been identified. Gaur has been recorded for the first time in Kashmir which is now extinct there. All these species including the wild sheep continued to occur during the megalithic period.

Bos, the Indian humped cattle mostly inhabiting the tropical countries was named as *Bos indicus* by Linneaus[4] and non-humped cattle was given the name *Bos taurus*. According to Rutimeyer[5] the humped cattle-*bos indicus* Linn, inhabiting the tropical countries is

1. Sankalia, H.D. and others, *From History to Prehistory at Nevasa*, Poona, 1960.
2. Nath B. 1966. Animals of prehistoric India and their affinities with those of the Western Asiatic Countries. *Records of Indian Museum, Vol. 59* (Part 4), Calcutta, 1966.
3. Nath B. *op.cit.*
4. Linnaeus, C. *Systema naturae* (ed X.), Stockholm. Linnaeus, C. 1788. *Systema Naturae* (ed. XIII), lipsiae, 1758.
5. Rutimeyer, L. Fauna of Swiss lake-dwellings — *Nouv. Mem. Soc. Helvet. Zurich*, 1862.

from very early times the sole type of domestic cattle of Asia and Africa and has undergone much less structural modification than the European forms. Duerst[1] and Prasad[2] felt that the short-horned type originated as a result of the "decline of cattle breeding" and is not to be considered as a new race. The long-horned humped cattle is considered to be the descendent of the Siwalik Nerbuddah Ox-*Bos Namadicus* Falconer.

The Urial sheep, *Ovis Vignei* Blyth, which extends all along the Harappan civilization area is supposed to be the ancestor of domestic sheep.

It is generally believed that the Indian buffalo is the direct lineal descendant of the gigantic *Bubalas palaeindicus* Falcover of Siwalik hills.

C. THE BURIALS

SKELETON NO. 1 - CANIS - WILD DOG (Pl. XVII)

A complete skeleton of a dog is found in pit 7 between peg number XXX' and XXIIIx' in the eastern sector of BZH-1 (1962). The pit is situated on the south-western corner of the trench. Major portion of the pit is on the plan while a portion of it occurs both in the western as well as in the southern section. The pit is cut in layer 9 and sealed by layer 8 with its top at the depth of 1.70 m from the present surface level. The maximum length of the pit available on the plan is 0.975m while the maximum breadth is 0.625 m.

The in-situ position of the skeleton suggests the sleeping posture of the animal. It is resting on its left side with its snout just touching the phalanges of the right front leg. The skeleton lying in the north south direction with its skull towards the north is more or less in articulated condition with few ribs and vertebrae lying disturbed.

---

1. Duerst, J.U., Animal Remains from the Excavation at Anau. *Exploration in Turkestan, Prehistoric Civilization of Anau,* Washington, 1908.
2. Prasad, B., Animal Remains from Harappa. *Mem. Archl. Survey of India,* No. 51. Delhi, 1936.

The skeleton is at the depth of 0.275 m from the top of the pit. Distal and proximal ends are not in the same level. The skeleton is lying on the slope with the hind portion on a higher and the front portion on a lower level. The pelvic region is at the depth of 1.85 m while the top of the skull is at the depth of 2.0 m from the present surface level.

Except for the left half of the pelvic girdle and left ribs nearly all the parts are visible in in-situ condition.

The skull is in fairly good state of preservation except for fractures on the premaxilla, caused due to the pressure of the earth. All the teeth in the upper and lower jaw are intact including the canines. The mandible is slightly damaged and very fragile. Frontal, parietal, zygomatic process of the squamosal and lachrymal bones are intact and in fairly good condition. Nasal bone is partly damaged.

So far as the vertebral column is concerned atlas, axis and most of the cervical vertebrae are present though they are not in their articulated condition. Almost all the caudal vertebrae are missing.

The right scapula is very fragile and broken, while the left is only partly visible and disturbed from its proper position.

Nearly all the ribs of the right side are present in broken and fragile state.

Right humerus is in its proper articulated position but is broken at the centre of the shaft. Both distal and proximal ends are intact and in fairly good condition. Left humerus is not visible.

Right radius and ulna are present in articulated condition with the condyle of the right humerus. Distal end of the right ulna is broken. Only few carpals, metacarpals and phalanges of the right fore limb are present scattered here and there.

Left radius and ulna are not visible.

Right half of the pelvic girdle is in its proper position but is broken and very fragile. Right iliac is broken into two at the centre while ischium and pubic regions have also developed cracks. Left hip bone is not visible.

Right femur is in good condition with its head near the right actabular cavity. Distal end is intact. Patella is missing. Right tibia and fibula are in articulated condition and in fairly good state of preservation. Astragalus, calcaneum, cuneiform, cuboid bones and phalanges of the right hind leg are present.

Left femur, tibia and fibula are partly visible in their disturbed position. Three of the metatarsals are lying away from the right tibia and fibula.

The bottom of the pit has not yet been reached.

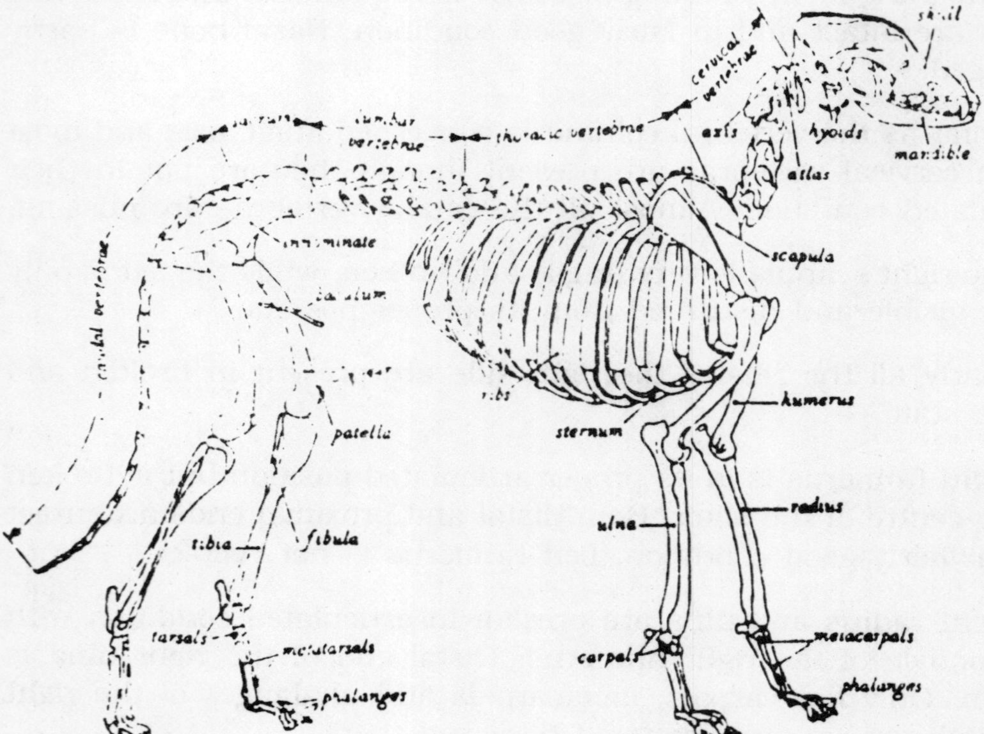

DOMESTIC DOG
Canis familiaris

SKELETON NO. 2 - DOG

A skeleton probably of a dog is found in a small pit cut nearly in the centre of a big pit numbered as 1 in the south-western quadrant of trench A1 of BZH-4 (1962). Pit 1 is cut in layer 6 at the depth of 1.68 m from the present surface level and is sealed by layer 5. The top of the pit containing the skeleton is at the depth of 1.70 m from the present surface level. It is plastered with 'Chunam" all around its inner sides. The pit is circular with the diameter of 0.90m. Filling of the pit consists of clay with an abundance of ashy material.

The skeleton is lying near the western fringe of the pit with its skull towards north facing west. The skeleton is resting on its right back in more or less articulated condition, with hind legs and pelvis region slightly disturbed. The front and hind legs are bent with the lower extremities of both touching each other. At the first sight the skeleton gives an impression of a running dog. Maximum length of the skeleton in in-situ condition (from vault of the skull to the ischium) is 0.625 m and the maximum breadth is 0.25 m.

Skull:- The skull is represented only by tiny fragments lying loose due to the ashy filling of the pit. The whole skeleton is very fragile and hardly anything worth studying can be lifted. Only the left half of the skull is visible. Frontal bone is completely missing along with the upper jaw, while the left temporal is pressed inside. Maxillary and premaxillary bones are badly damaged. A piece of left parietal is left. The eye orbit is not at all visible except for a piece of zygomatic process. Third premolar of the left upper jaw is present. Except for the three left lower molars all the other teeth of the left mandible are missing.

The auricular condyle is present while the tip of the coronoid process is broken.

Vertebral Column:- The vertebral column is in fairly good articulated condition though some caudal vertebrae are missing. The two present are lying disturbed from their proper position. All the vertebrae are extremely fragile and spines of most of them are broken. The cervical and thoracic are comparatively better than the lumbar and caudal. Fragments of ribs from both the sides are visible. Some of the rib fragments from the left side have mounted on the thoracic region of the vertebral column. Most of the pieces of ribs are disturbed from their actual position.

Scapula:- Left scapula is present and is very fragile. Glenoid cavity of both the sides are quite intact. The spine including the acromion process of the left scapula is broken. The coracoid process as well as the inferior and superior angles are damaged.

Forelimbs:- Both the right and left humerii are in proper articulated position. The upper and lower extremities of the left humerus are in fairly good state of preservation but that of the right humerus is in damaged condition. Both the humerii are lying side by side. Radius and ulna of both the sides are broken into several pieces and are very fragile. Their lower extremities are completely missing. Left radius and ulna have mounted on the tibiae, while that of the right side are lying disturbed.

Phalanges from the left fore-limbs are present, while from the right fore-limb, only four metacarpals are present. Cuboids are missing.

Hind limbs:- Left femur is represented by two pieces (upper and lower extremities) while the middle portion of the shaft is missing. The head of the left femur is dislodged from the acetabular cavity of the left side. The right femur is more or less in proper position. Its medial and lateral condyles including the popliteal surface are broken. It has also cracked at the centre of the shaft. Only the upper extremity and the upper half of the shaft of left tibia are present. The remains of tibia are extremely fragile. Right tibia is not visible and both the fibulae are missing. Astragalus, calcaneum, cuboid and phalanges of the hind legs are missing.

The left half of the pelvis is in badly damaged and fragile condition. It has broken into three big pieces apart from several cracks on them. Above the acetabular cavity the ilium has broken

into pieces. Similarly below the acetabular cavity ischium has also broken and separated from its right half.

The bottom of the pit has not been reached. After lifting this skeleton the pit is further scooped out and nearly 0.15 m below this skeleton another animal skeleton (probably the same as the previous one) is found lying in articulated condition. It is towards the eastern side of the pit. This skeleton could not be fully exposed and lifted due to incliment whather and lack of time.

MULE DEER
Odocoileus hem[illegible]nus

SKELETON NO. 3 WOLF
(Pl. XVIII)

The animal skeleton is found in pit 7 of the north east quadrant of A-11, BZH-3 (1962). The pit 7 is sealed by another pit numbered 5.

The skeleton is completely charred at various places on is lying at the depth of 1.85 m from the present surface level. The pit containing the skeleton is on the north eastern corner of the trench and is filled with d ashy deposit.

The skeleton is lying on its left side in the north-east, south-west direction with the skull towards north facing east. Legs are towards the eastern section.

Bones in the periphery of pelvic region are completely charred. Most of the vertebrae, some of the ribs, both the femurii, pelvic girdle, upper ends of both the tibia and fibula, lower end of right humerus, upper half of the right radius and ulna are charred.

The skeleton is lying in more or less articulated condition. Most of the parts are extremely fragile, damaged and loose due to the ashy deposit of the pit.

Some of the charred vertebrae and ribs have been collected for C-14 test.

The skull is represented by numerous small fragments and is extremely fragile. The mandible is also broken into several pieces and hardly anything worth studying can be lifted intact. Two canines are present. Both the scapulae are practically missing except for their impression on the earth. The ribs are broken into small fragments and not a single piece is complete. Right humerus is intact at the proximal end but is broken at the distal end. Both the extremities are safe. Left humerus is also broken at its proximal end while the rest of the portion is in fairly good state of preservation.

Right radius in broken at the middle of the shaft, but the extremities are intact. Left radius is intact. Right ulna is represented by two pieces while the middle portion of its shaft is missing. Carpals and metacarpals, of the fore-limbs are present in fairly good condition. The pelvis region is completely charred and is represented by several small pieces. Right femur is broken into three pieces. Shaft is intact but the head and the extremities are separate. Left femur is broken at the upper end separating the head from the shaft. A part of the upper half of left femur is lying below the vertebral column. Left patella is present in its proper position while the right one is missing.

Right tibia and fibula are broken from the middle. Their proximal and distal ends are in good state of preservation. Left tibia is broken at its distal end and the left fibular bone is broken at the middle. Right calcaneus and cuboids are intact. Left tarsals and phalanges are well preserved.

The skeleton lying at the bottom of the pit is 0.625 m in length (measured from the vault to the end of pelvis) in in-situ condition.

SKELETON NO. 4 - Skulls of wild Dogs. (Cluster of skulls and other fragmentary bones along with an antler) (Pl. XV)

A number of dog skulls along with other fragmentary bones and an antler horn, are found dumped with stone pieces in pit-1 of the south-eastern sector of the quadrant B-II, BZH-3(1962). The pit is situated on the south-western corner of the trench. Two pits in the shape of numerical '8' have been cut in the floor sealed by layer 8. Top of the pit is at the depth of 2.075 m from the present surface level. The pit does not seem to be a refuge pit as it is dovoid of any ashy material. Though the skulls are lying scattered mostly devoid of their respective mandibles but surprisingly a portion of vertebral column is attached in articulated condition with nearly all the skulls. Some of the long bones and hip bones have got absolutely no mark of any damage.

In in-situ condition the following parts are visible :-

Five skulls, eight mandibles, one pelvis (including the left and right hip bones), one left hip bone, two scapula, an antler horn and many fragmentary limb bones. Few complete and broken ribs are also present.

To start form the western end of the pit the first skull is in good state of preservation and articulated with it are three vertebrae. Of all the skulls it is the only one where both the mandibles are intact. Except for the first and second incisors of the right upper jaw all the teeth in lower and upper jaw are intact. The skull is resting on its left side. Premaxilla, nasal, frontal, parietal and squamosal bones are intact. Mandibles are in fairly good condition. Right zygomatic process is missing.

In front of the first skull is lying one rib and the horn of the antler. The horn is broken at the top and has got two more branches besides the main. Four fragmentary ribs are lying near the horn. Overriding the second branch of the horn is another skull. Two vertebrae are attached in damaged condition to the foramen magnum of this second skull. The second skull is resting on its right side devoid of its mandible. Left Zygomatic process, sphenoid and squamosal are broken. From the left upper jaw three molars, two premolars, one canine and one incisor are visible. Premaxilla is slightly damage. A third skull is lying away from the supra-occipital region of the second skull. It is resting on its right side and is facing north-west. A piece of vertebral column containing eight verterbrae, is attached to the occipital condyle of the third skull. Spines of some of the vertebrae are broken. Except for the snout which is not visible the skull is in fairly good state of preservation. Left zygomatic bones is intact. Three molars and one premolars of the left side are visible. Frontal, parietal and left squamosal are intact.

A portion of vertebral column containing eight vertebrae is lying below the snout of the second skull.

The fourth skull is lying in the south-eastern corner of the pit *i.e.*, south-east of the second skull. It is lying upside down and is in good state of preservation. Two canines, one right premolar and two incisors of the left side are present. Palatal aspect is visible. Zygomatic process of both the sides are present. Palate is intact. Occipital condyle and foramen magnum are in good condition. Five vertebrae are attached to the foramen magnum of this skull and are in proper articulated condition. Spines of the vertebrae are damaged.

Two mandibles, one over the other are lying towards the south of the fourth skull. They belong to the two sides, right one overriding the left. Except for the damaged condyle and angular process, right mandible is more or less intact. Canine, two premolars and three molars are present.

Fifth skull is lying towards the north-east of the third skull. It is resting on its right side, facing east. Only a portion of the left premaxilla and left squamosal is visible. A long chain of twenty vertebrae are overriding the skull lengthwise. Spines of most of the vertebrae are intact. Left zygomatic process of the fifth skull is missing and so also the second left premolar. With the skull are eight vertebrae in articulated condition but damaged.

Between the fifth and third skull is lying a chain of another vertebral column consisting of eight vertebrae. It is passing below the vertebral column of the third skull. Between the third and fifth skull right mandible is lying. Its major portion is hidden by the third skull. Angular process and condylar region are intact. Molars are in good condition. In front of the third skull is lying one complete pelvis along with the iliac portion of another hip bone. Ventral aspect of the pelvis is visible. Ilium, ischium and pubic bones of both the sides are intact though they have cracked at several places. Symphysis is damaged while both the acetabular cavities are intact.

Two mandibles are lying towards the west of the above mentioned pelvis. Only the angular process of one of them is visible. The second one which belongs to the right is quite intact. Except for the third and fourth premolar all other parts are intact.

Fragmentary ribs and long bones are lying near the above mentioned mandible. Extremities of most of the long bones are damaged. Near the vertebral column of the fifth skull is lying a femur with its intact head and broken shaft. In front of the fourth skull is one scapula with its glenoid cavity intact. Just touching the glenoid cavity is another complete left mandible. On the right of the fourth skull, a right femur and a piece of tibia are lying. Extremities of the femur are quite intact. A humerus with intact shaft and extremeties is lying near the scapula. Below the humerus is a broken distal and of femur. A radius, ulna and fibula are lying towards the east of humerus. Near the fifth skull are several broken shafts and one femur with damaged extremities. Below this femur is another mandible with its only canine, premolars and premaxilla visible. A hip bone cracked near the acetabular cavity is lying near the above mentioned mandible. Ilium and ischium are quite intact. A scapula is partly visible towards the north of the hip bone. A humerus, radius and ulna are lying near the scapula. Lower extremities of radius and ulna and the head of the humerus are missing.

Diameter of pit-1 containing the congregation of bones is roughly 1.32 m while the diameter of pit-2 is 1.20 m.

Both the pits were further scooped out. Pit 2 yielded nothing while at the bottom of the pit 1 another antler horn is found.

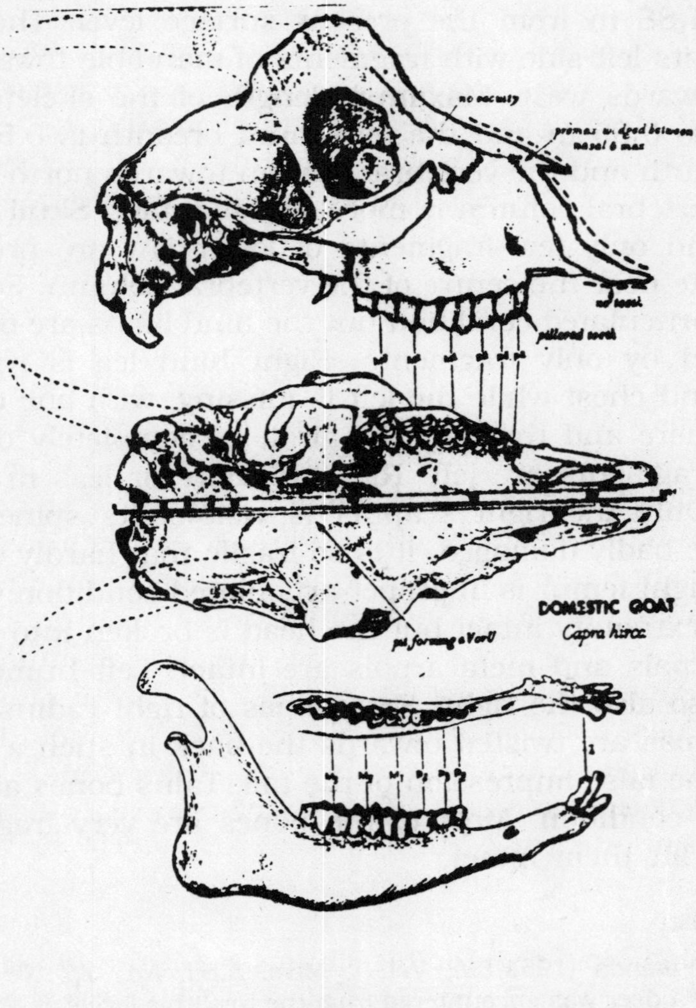

SKELETON NO. 5 - Ibex-(Capra falconeri) (Pl. XVI)

An animal skeleton (most probably that of an Ungulata) is lying in pit 15 of south-eastern sector of B-6, BZH-3(1962). The pit is circular with a radius of 0.525 m and is cut in layer 5 sealed by layer 4b. The pit is in the south-western corner of the trench. The top of the pit is at the depth of 1.56 m and the skeleton is at the depth of 1.88 m from the present surface level. The skeleton is resting on its left side with fragments of mandible towards east and the tail towards west. Maximum length of the skeleton in in-situ condition is 0.85 m and the maximum breadth is 0.55m Legs are towards south and the vertebral column towards north running east to west. Vertebral column is more or less intact. Skull is practically missing and only few fragments of lower jaw are present in disturbed state near the centre of the vertebral column. Fore-limbs are in proper articulated condition but the hind limbs are disturbed and represented by only fragments. Right hind leg is lying over the stomach and chest while the left is missing, with one or two pieces scattered here and there. Pelvic girdle is completely damaged and only few fragments are left. Ribs are more or less in their proper position. Only the right scapula is visible. Its spine and lateral borders are badly damaged. It is so fragile that hardly anything can be lifted. Right femur is in proper articulated condition with its shaft and lower extremity intact but the head is broken into pieces. Right radius, carpals and metacarpals are intact. Left humerus is complete and so also the right. Extremities of right radius are broken. Atlas and axis are twisted towards the back in such a fashion that they give the false impression of the tail. Talus bones are present in fairly good condition. Most of the bones are very fragile and it is difficult to lift them intact.

Nagarjunakonda (1954-60), Vol. I, *Mem. A.S.I. No., 75*, New Delhi, 1975. Burial of a deer was encountered from the Neolithic levels at Nagarjunakonda. In an irregular pit measuring 2.39m x 1.83m, depth 0.46m. filled with ask and blackish soil skeletal remains of deer, with skull missing, were recovered. The skeleton was put in north-south orientation and bore no cut marks. Association of pottery and few antiquibes with the burial suggest some ritualistic performance.

SKELETON NO. 6

In the baulk facing east (looking west) between the two quadrants falling between peg Nos. XXIX'-XXIX, skeletal remains of a dog are found in a circular grave-pit. It cannot be said as to in which layer the pit has been cut because the top of the pit could not be detected while cutting the baulk. Only half of the pit is present while the other half has been most probably cut by the pit dug for animal burial No.1 (Dog.).

The skeleton is lying in north-south direction in articulated condition. Skull is towards north and caudal region is towards south. The skeleton is resting on its left side. Unfortunately the skull is missing except for three molars and two canines which are attached to small fragments of maxilla. No trace of upper jaw is available. The skeleton is lying in slightly slanting position with the pelvic region on a higher level than the fore limbs and skull fragments. Pelvic bone is at the depth of 1.83m form the present surface level while the skull region is at the depth of 2.28m, Maximum length of the skeleton in in-situ condition is 0.65m.

Vertebral column is more or less in articulated condition except for few thoracic vertebrae that are missing. Fore-limbs are in stretched condition. Left humerus is articulated with the glenoid cavity. It is in two pieces as it has broken near the head. Left radius and ulna are in good condition and complete. Right humerus is represented only by a piece of lower extremely. Right radius and ulna are present in articulated condition. Phalanges are totally missing. Scapula is in badly damaged condition and has broken into several pieces, with its right glenoid cavity totally missing.

Almost all the ribs are present either in full or in pieces. Right half of the pelvic bone is present in damaged state. Right acetabulum is broken.

Hind limbs are stretched towards the fore-limbs. Both the femur are present with their heads missing. Shaft and lower extremities are intact. Right tibia is present in full while rest of the bones of the hind limbs are missing.

Maximum length of the grave pit, north-south is 0.85m.

SKELETON NO. 7

Skeletal remains of an animal (probably Wolf?) are found in pit 5a of the dquadrant BZH-4(63)-A4-A5-. The pit is quite big in size and is not a grave pit. It has been cut in layer 8a sealed by pit 5 and layer 4. The pit 5a is peculiar in shape. The skeleton is lying in the north eastern corner of the pit at the depth of 3.83m from the present surface level. It is lying on its left side with its forelimbs towards north and hind limbs towards south. Vertebral column is towards west while the legs are pointing towards east. Maximum length of the skeleton in in-situ condition north south is 0.60m from pelvic region to phalanges of left fore limb. Almost all the parts present are in perfect articulated condition.

Skull is represented by a piece of zygomatic bone only.

Of the left fore limb only a portion of it is visible as it is hidden below the right fore-limb. Left humerus is not visible. Lower half of radius and ulna are visible and have broken at their distal ends. Left carpals, metacarpals and phalanges are present. Left fore limb is twisted towards the skull region. Right fore limb is in perfect articulated condition with all the bones present in fairly good condition. Head of humerus which has separated from the shaft is articulated with the glenoid cavity. Right radius and ulna are in articulation with the distal end of humerus. Carpals, metacarpals, phalanges and claws are present. Only right scapula is visible. It has cracked from several places and is very fragible. Vertebral column is in articulated condition. Atlas, axis and caudal vertebrae are missing. Thoracic and lumbar vertebrae are present but their spines have broken.

Almost all the ribs are present mostly in pieces.

Pelvis is in badly damaged condition. Right half of the pelvic bone is totally missing. Left had has also broken into several pieces particularly at the acetabular point.

Right femur is represented only by its lower third. Right tibia and fibula are in articulated condition. Tibia has cracked at the upper end while fibula has broken into three pieces Right astragalus is prominent.

Tarsals, meta-tarsals and phalanges are present in proper position.

Left femur is present in articulated condition. Only the lower end of left tibia is visible while rest of its parts and fibula are hidden by the right femur, tibia and fibula. Left foot-bones are present in good condition.

With this skeleton some foreign bones are also present. Towards the north of right fore limb is present lower half of a humerus, radius, ulna and phalanges belonging to that of a dog. These parts are in articulated condition. Near the skull region and from below the right scapula is jutting out the lower half of tibia and fibula and with their distal ends are articulated astragalus and calcaneum pieces. Head of another femur is also visible below these bones.

Near the skull piece is lying a broken distal end of a femur and a piece of fibula. It is possible that these parts might belong to another animal which may be lying just below this skeleton.

Below the phalanges of right hind limbs just touching the claw bones is lying a single big vertebra probably that of an Ibex or some big animal of that size.

DOMESTIC SHEEP *Ovis aries*

SKELETON NO. 8
(Below animal burial No. 2)

Skeletal remains of another dog are found in grave pit 2 of quadrant BZH-4, A-1 when the pit was further scooped out. The pit has been sealed by layer 5. The same pit yielded skeleton of a dog, on its western half during 1962 excavations.

After 0.075m of the ashy material mixed with stone pieces was scooped out, another skeleton of a dog is found, this time in the western half of the grave pit.

This skeleton is also lying in the same fashion as the previous one. Both were lying parallel to each other in a stepwise fashion.

The skeleton is lying in north south direction with the skull towards north and the caudal region towards south. It is resting on its right side with the limbs towards west and vertebral columns towards east.

Fortunately the skeleton is more or less complete except for heavy cracks and breakages of the bones. Lower ends of all the fore limbs have been placed above each other,

The skeleton is lying at the depth of 2.013m from the present surface level. Snout and end of the limbs are lying at a higher level while the pectoral portion is at a lower level, 2.075m and 2.018m respectively below surface.

Maximum length of the skeleton from snout to caudal end is 0.65m while maximum breadth is 0.38m in-situ condition.

While burying the dog its skull was twisted side-wise to make an angle roughly of 80° with the atlas so that it is mostly resting on the occipital region with the jaw ends placed in norma-occipitalis position.

Both the maxilla are in good condition with nearly all the teeth present.

Upper jaw is heavily damaged and the canines are missing. Zygomatic bone has also broken into pieces. Eye-orbits are damaged. Maxilla is also badly damaged and is extremely fragile.

Vertebral column is in perfectly articulated condition and all the vertebrae right from the atlas to caudal are present. Atlas, axis, and thoracic vertebrae are crushed and it is hardly possible to lift anything intact.

Scapula is broken into several small fragments.

Both the fore-limbs are in articulated condition and have been stretched towards the hind legs. Left humerus is intact. Upper and lower extremities are safe but the shaft has cracked into several pieces. Right humerus is lying below the left and is thus not visible and their lower extremeties are damaged.

Left radius and ulna are intact. All the carpals, metacarpals and phalanges of the fore-limbs are present.

Almost all the ribs are in their position but have broken into several pieces. Hip-bone is badly damaged, left iliac bone is intact but the right one is broken, pubic bone has also cracked, ischium is intact. Both the hind limbs are in articulated condition. Head of left femur is broken, distal end is intact, shaft has cracked into several pieces. Right femur is badly damaged at the distal end, and shaft region. Head is intact and articulated with the acetabular cavity. Left tibia and fibula have broken into two pieces at the upper third where as right tibia and fibula are intact. Astragalus of left leg is intact and visible. Astragalus, calcaneum and phalanges of the right leg are lying below those of the left.

SKELETON NO. 9

In quadrant BZH3, B-6, (south eastern sector) grave pit 15 sealed by layer 5a was further scooped out. After lifting the Ibex skeletal remains exposed during 1962 season (animal skeleton No. 5) in the same grave pit at a higher level, at the depth of 2.175m from the present surface level, a number of loose bones belonging to different animals are encountered inside the pit.

It seems that the pieces of bones were dumped in the pit after the flesh was consumed. All the bones except for the piece of a horn, are concentrated towards the northern half of the pit.

The cluster contains two major portions of antler, in highly damaged and fragile condition, piece of a verebral column (probably that of a dog.), containing atleast ten articulated vertebrae, piece of a jaw (goat) containing five teeth, one scapula with its glenoid cavity intact, two humerus, three radii, two ulnae, one femur and pieces of several ribs. Apart form these, piece of another damaged scapula, few vertebrae, a piece or two of limb bones are also jutting out in the pit.

The animals represented in the pit are mostly stag, dog, sheep, and goat. The bones have been dumped along with several stone pieces. Pit filling mostly consists of ashy clay and stone pieces.

SKELETON NO. 10

In quadrant BZH-1, between peg Nos. XXX'-XXIIIX' skeletal remains of a pup is found just near and parallel to the southern section facing north. This animal has been buried at a lower level (2.33m from the surface), than the animal skeleton No.1 found during 1962 season in the same pit.

On the plan maximum length of the pit is 1.30m and breadth is 1.20m. Little away form the centre of the pit towards south eastern corner a big post hole is present.

The skeleton is lying in east west direction, with its skull towards east, snout pointing towards north east and caudal region toward west. Back is towards south and limbs are towards north. It is resting on its right side. Maximum length of the skeleton in in-situ state, from maxillary teeth to the caudal end is 0.60m.

Unfortunately the skeleton is in badly damaged condition. Skull and limbs are particularly damaged. Both the maxilla are present. Left parts of the skull particularly zygomatic process and eye orbits are totally smashed. Skull has broken into several small fragments and it is hardly possible to lift it intact. Occipital region is in fairly good condition. All the teeth are present.

Vertebral column is very much intact with almost all the vertebrae present including the caudal ones and in articulated condition. Spines of some are broken. Almost all the ribs of the left side are intact and in articulated condition. Left scapula is in perfectly good condition with its margins and spines intact. With its glenoid cavity is articulated the undamaged left humerus. Left radius is represented by its upper third, with its proximal end intact. Left ulna is in good condition.

Right fore limb is almost hidden. A portion of right humerus is jutting out from below just to the right of the left scapula. Phalanges of both the forelimbs are totally missing. Pelvic bone is in fairly good condition. Only the half of both the hip bones are visible. Left hip bone has cracked into several pieces. Of the right hind limb proximal end (head) and shaft portion of the femur is present. Right femur has broken into three pieces. Tibia and fibula of both limbs are totally missing. Phalanges of the left hind limbs are lying just near the distal end of right femur. They are also incomplete. Bottom of the grave pit is on top of layer 2.

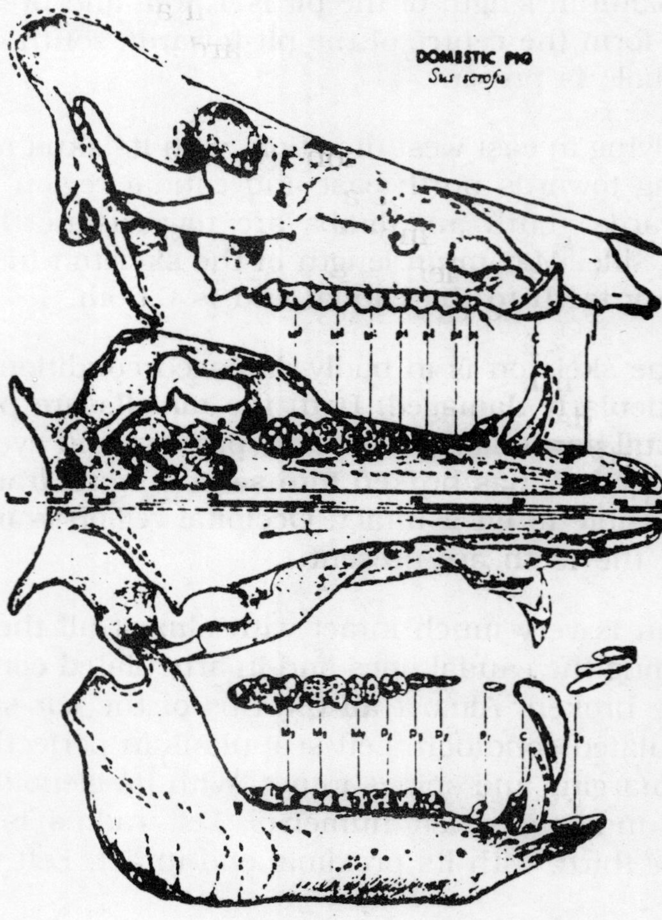

SKELETON NO. 11

Skeletal remains of a dog are found just below the animal skeleton No. 7 in pit 5a sealed by 8a in badly twisted condition. Only about 0.05m of the pit deposit was between the two skeletons. From the position of the skeleton it seems that the dog was put in supine position resting on its back and with the limbs upwards drawn towards each other i.e. to the stomach region, and with the skull hanging on its left side.

Skull is intact. It is resting on the left side on norma verticalis position looking towards north west. Mandibles are towards north east. Right eye-orbit, all the teeth, zygomatic bone, zygomatic process, maxilla, right parietal and occipital regions, all are intact. On the right maxilla, rudimentary third molar is present. Snout region is badly damaged and fragile. Major portion of the vertebral column is articulated with the skull. Beyond second thoracic vertebra it has twisted badly at right angles. Spines of most of the vertebrae are broken. Both the scapulae are present but disturbed from their position and in extremely fragile condition. Greater angles are damaged but glenoid cavities are intact. Most of the ribs are present in twisted condition, those of the right side riding over the vertebral column.

From the left fore-limb only the distal end of humerus is present, while rest of the parts are missing.

Distal half of the right humerus is present in articulation with right radius and ulna. Only few of the carpals, metacarpals and one or two phalanges of the right fore limb are present. Major portion of the pelvic bone is intact and in good condition. Both the acetabular cavities, ischiatic bones are present. Pubic region is badly damaged.

From the right hind limb only the femur is present. It is complete and slightly disturbed form its position. Anatomical neck is damaged. Left hind limb is totally missing. Shaft piece of right femur is lying near the ribs.

D. Special features of animal burials of Burzahom

1. Like human beings animals are also buried in regular circular pits inside the habitation area itself. Except skeleton no. 4 (cluster of skulls) others are in articulated condition. Skeleton no. 3 was more or less charred showing that probably a part inhumation process was performed. In case of skeleton no. 4 atleast five dog skulls mostly articulated with the major portion of their respective vertebral columns, have been dumped in a circular pit. Other parts of the body are also lying in the same pit, complete or in fragments.

2. Orientation of all the articulated skeletons are north-south with the skull towards north either facing west (skeleton no.2) or facing east (skeleton nos. 1 & 3) as in the case of human skeletons.

3. Skull or other parts of the pet animals have been buried with human skeletons in the same pit.

   Skull of a dog is found burried with human skeleton no.3 in the same pit at a higher level than the human skeleton. Ibex skull fragments, a piece of lower jaw treated with redochre and antlers are found with human skeleton no. 7 at different levels of the grave pit. Fragmentary bones of a goat are associated with skeleton no. 6.

4. Systematic burial of more than one animal or its fragments at different levels in the same grave pit were observed.

e.g.,

1. Animal skeleton Nos. 1 and 10.
2. Animal skeleton Nos. 2 and 8.
3. Animal skeleton Nos. 5 and 9.
4. Animal skeleton Nos. 7 and 11.

SELECT BIBLIOGRAPHY

Agarwal, D.P. 1982 Archaeology of India Scandinavian, Institute of Asian Studies, Monograph Series No. 46, London.

Agarwal, D.P. and Sheela Kusumgar, 1965-Radocarban dates of some neolithic and early historic Samples. Current Science, 34 No. 42-43 Bangalore.

Allchin, F.R. 1960 Piklihal, Excavations. Hyderabad.

Allichin, B and R. 1968-The Birth of Indian Civilization. Middlesex.

Ancient India No. 3, New Delhi.

Arne, T.J. Excavation at Shah Tepe Iran.

Basu, Anand, Pal, Anadi. 1980 - Human Remains form Burzahom Calcutta.

Binford, L.R., 1981 - *Bones; Ancient and Modern Myths*, New York

Bose, N.K. 1959 - 'Comparative Study of Civilization'. Man in India, Vol. 39 No. 3.

Bose, N.K. 1963 Progress of Anthropology & Archaeology; Fifty years of Science in India. Indian Science Congress, Calcutta.

Bose, N.K. 1965 - The People'. The Gazetter of India, Indian Union, Vol. I.

Brothwell, D.R. 1959 Digging up Bones, London.

Capriani, 1962. The Illustrated London, News, Feb. 3. London.

Cesare, Emiliani, 1960, Dating Human Evolution. The Evolution of Man, Vol. II.

Childe, V. Gordon 1937. Main Makes Himself. London.

Cornwall, I.W. 1956. Bones for the Archaeologists. London.

Dani, A.H. 1988 - Recent Archaeological Discoveries in Pakistan. UNESCO.

Dange, S.S. 1987 - Sacrifices in India, Concept and Evolution, Bombay.

Dey, A.K. Geology of India, National Book Trust, New Delhi.

De Morgan, 1924 -Prehistoric Man, London.

De Terra, and T.T. Paterson 1939. Studies in the Ice Age, in India and Associated Human Cultures, Washington.

Duerst, J.U. 1908. Animal remains from the excavation at Anau Exploration in Turkestan, Prehistoric Civilization of Anau. Washington.

Emergy, W.T. - 1963 - ' Dental Pathology and Archaeolgy'. Antiquity Vol. XXXVI, No. 148, Cambridge.

Gilman, H. 1982. On the Prehitoric Trephining and cranial amulets in North American Ethnology.

Guha, B.S. and Basu P.C. 1928-29' Report on Human Remains excavated at Mohenjodaro in 1928-29' Further Excavation at Mohenjodaro.

Guha, B.S. 1935 - 'Racial Affinities of the people of India', Census - 1931, Simla.

1937 - 'An outline of Racial Ethnology of India; An outline of the field science in India, Indian Science Congress, Calcutta.

Gupta, S.P. 1972 Disposal of the Dead and Physical Types in Ancient India. Delhi.

Gupta P., Dutta P.C. and Basu A. 1962 - 'Human Skeletal Remains from Harappa : Anthropological Survey of Indian Memoir No. 9, Calcutta.

Gupta P., Basu A. and Others, 'Ancient Human Remains' Anthropological Survey of India, Memoir No. 20, Calcutta.

Gupta P. 1975 - 'Human Remains in Indian Subcontinent during Pre and Protohistoric Periods'. Bio-anthropological research in India. Calcutta.

Hargreaves, H. 1929 - 'Excavation in Baluchistan'. *Memoris of the A.S.I. No. 35*, Calcutta.

Indian Archaeology 1959-60 A Review, New Delhi.

Indian Archaeology 1960-61 A Review, New Delhi.

Indian Archaeology 1962-63 A Review, New Delhi.

Indian Archaeology 1963-64 A Review, New Delhi.

Indian Archaeology 1964-65 A Review, New Delhi.

Indian Archaeology 1967-68 A Review, New Delhi.

Indian Archaeology 1968-69 A Review, New Delhi.

James Mellart. *1964 - Illustrated London News, Feb. 15-22.* London,

Josef Augusta, 1960 - *'Prehistoric Man'* London.

J. Gourerich, 1965 - *'Recorded in Clay'* - Abbottempo. Book 1, London.

Johnstan T.B. *etc.* 1958 - Gray's Anatomy. London.

Khazanchi, T.N. 1976. Pit - Dwellere of Buzahom - *The Illustrated Weakly of India.*

Khazanchi T.N. 1977, North-Western Neolithic Cultures of India, *Indian Institute of Advanced Studies, News letters 7 & 8.* Simla.

Krogman, Wilton M. 1962, *The Human Skeleton in Forensic Medicine.* Springfield.

Lal B.B. and S.P. Gupta (ed) 1984, *Frontiers of Indian Civilization.* Delhi.

Linnaeus, C. 1758. *System Naturae* (ed.x) Stockhorm.

Morgan, Jacques, De. 1924. *Prehistoric Man.* A General Outline of Prehistory.

Nagarajarao M.S. and Malhotra K.C. 1965 - *The Stone Age Hill Dwellers of Tekkalkota;* Poona.

Nath, B. 1966. Animals of Prehistonic India and their Affinities with those of the Western Afiatic Countries. *Records of the Indian Museum*, Vol. 59 (Part 4). Calcutta.

Oakley, K.P. etc. 1959. Contribution on Trepanning or trephination in ancient and modern times, Man, Vol. LIX No. 133. London.

Pal, Anadi. 1981 - 'Dental health in Ancient India', Journal of the Indian Anthropological Society, Vol. 16, No. 2.

Pande B.M. 1969 - 'Adim Kashmir ke "garta-vasi", (Pit-dwellers of prehistoric Kashmir : in Hindi), Samskriti, Dr. Adityanath Jha Abhinandand Grantha, Vol. III, Delhi.

___do____ 1970 - 'The Neolithic in Kashmir : new discoveries' The Anthropologist, University of Delhi, Vol. XVII, nos. 1 & 2.

____do____ 1971 - 'Neolithic hunting -scene on a stone -slab from Burzahom, Kashmir', Asian Perspectives, University of Hawaii, Vol. XIX, 1971 (1973).

____do____ 1972 - 'A neolithic "tectiform" from Burzahom, District Srinagar. Kashmir', Journal of the Indian Anthropological Society Calcutta, Vol. XXXII, pt. 2.

____do____1973 - 'Kucch kshya nahin hota' (Nothing decays : in Hindi), Dinamana.

____d0____ 1990 - "Magico - religious practices of the Neolithic people of Burzahom, Kashmir', Himalaya, past and present, Almora.

Parry, T.W. 1928 - 'Holes in the Skulls of Prehistonic Man and Their Significance' Archaeological Journal, LXXXV : 1-12.

Piggott. Stuart (ed.) 1961. The Dawn of Civilization. New York.

Possehl G.L. 1982 - Harappan Civilization, Oxford.

Prasad, B. 1936. Animal Remains from Harappa - Mem. Archaeological Survey of India No. 51, Delhi.

Rutimeyer, L. 1862. Fauna of Swiss Lake dwellings - Nouv. Men. Soc. Helvet. Zurich.

Sarkar, S.S. 1959-The Aboriginal Races of India' Calcutta 1960.

____do____ 'Human Skeletal remains from Brahamagiri'. Bulletin of Deptt. of Anthropology 9 (i) Calcutta.

____do____ 1964 - 'Ancient Races of Baluchistan', Punjab and Sind. Calcutta.

Sen, D.K. - 1967 ' Ancient Races of India and Pakistan - A study of method : Ancient India, Nos. 20 & 21 : New Delhi.

Sewell, S. and Guha B.S. - 1931 'Human Remains'. Mohenjodaro and the Indus Civilization.

Sewell, S. and Guha B.S. - 1929 - 'Reports on the bones excavated at Nal' Archaeological Survey of India Memoir No. 35, Calcutta.

Sewell. S. and Guha B.S. 1931 - 'Report on a Collection of bones made by Aurel Stein in Makran'. A.S.I. Memoir No. 43.

Sisson, S. 1967. The anatomy of the domestic animals, Tokyo.

Sharma, A.K., - 1967 - 'Neolithic human burials from Burzahom - Kashmir' Journal of the Orient Institute Vol. XVI, No. 3, Baroda.

____d0____ 1968 - 'Neolithic Animal Burials from Burzahom - A Neolithic Settlement in Kashmir' Journal of the Oriental Institute, Baroda, Vol. XVIII, Nos. 1 & 2, Baroda.

____do____ 1969 - Kalibangan Human Skeletal remains : an osteo Archaeological approach; Journal of the Oriental Institute Vol. XIX, No. 102, Baroda.

____do____ 1980 - ' Excavation at Gufkrat' Puratattva No. 11, New Delhi.

____do____ 1980-81. Animal Boses-from Gufkral-Evidence of Human and non-human activities. Puratattva No. 12. New Delhi.

____do___ _ 1990 'Animal Remains from Surkotada', Excavation at Surkotada. New Delhi.

____do____ 1994 ' Animal Remains from Bhagwanpura', Excavation at Bhagwanpura, New Delhi.

Singh, R.L. (ed) India, A Regional Geography, Varanasi, 1971.

Stacul Giorgio 1975 - 'The fractional burial custom in the Swat Valley and some Connected Problems', in East and West New Series Vol. 25, Nos. 3-4.

Thapar B.K. (1985) Recent Archaeological Discoveries in India (Unesco Publication).

Trotter, M. and G.C. Gleser. 1952 Estimation of Stature from long bones of Amercian whites and Nagroes. *American Journal of Physical* Anth. 10.

Wadia, D.N. 1939. Geology of India. London.

Wells, Calvin - 1964 - *Bones, Bodies and Diseases*. London.

Wheeler, R.E.M. 'Harappa', *Ancient India*, No. 3, New Delhi.

Wheeler, R.E.M. 1966 - *Civilization of the Indus Valley and Beyond* London.

Wilder H.H. 1920 *A Laboratory Mannual of Anthropometry*, Philadelphia.

Wooley Leonard C - 1934 - *Ur Excavation II, The Royal Cemetery'*. London.

Wooley Leonard C. - 1950 - *'Ur of the Chaldees'*. London.

Zeuner, F.E. 1950 *Dating the Past*. London.

Zittel, Karl A. Von. 1925. *The Text Book of Palaeontology*, London.

INDEX

O

P

Q

R

S

T

U

V

W

Z

ILLUSTRATIONS

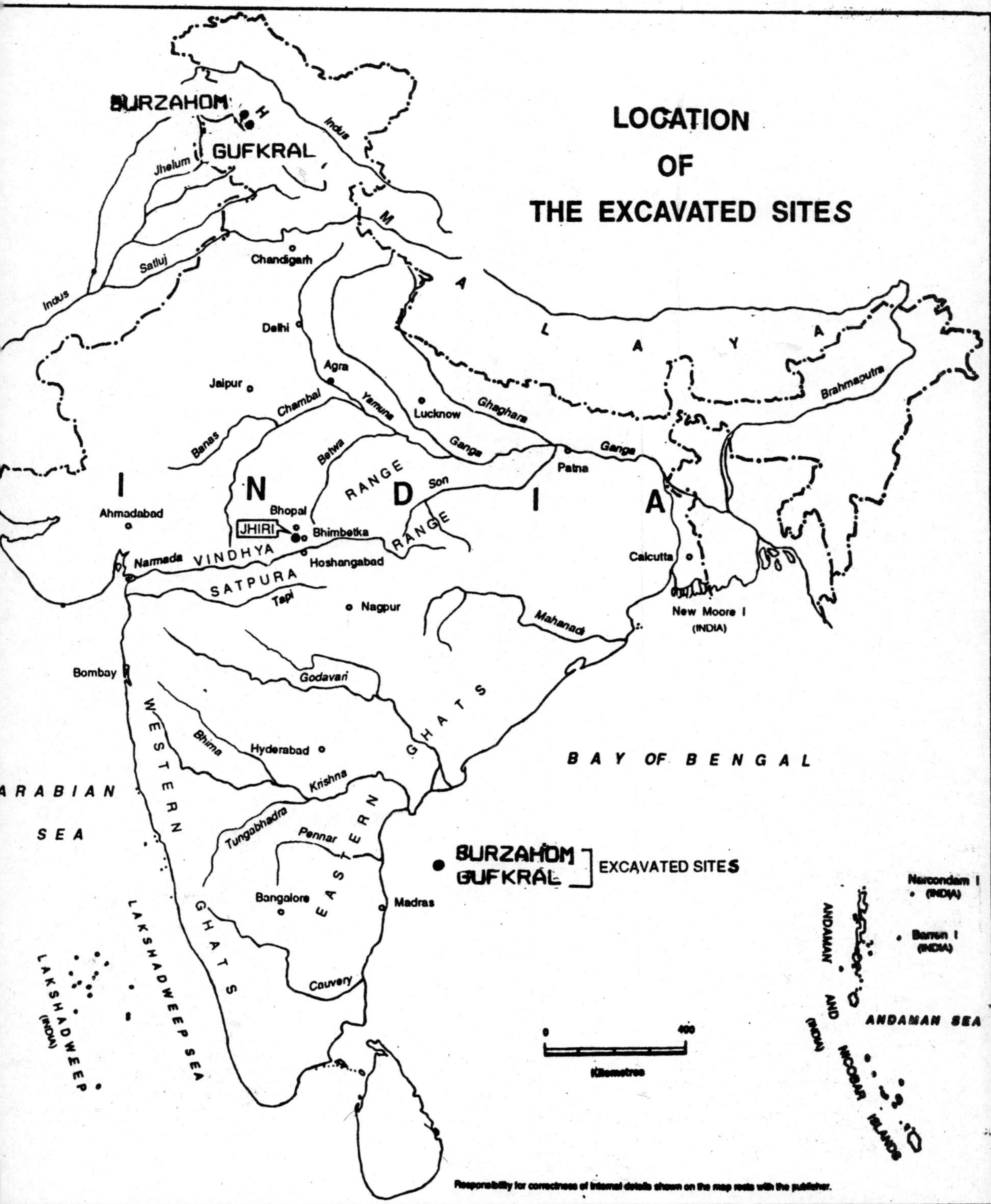

...upon Survey of India map with the permission of the Surveyor General of India

© Government of India Copyright, 1984

...rritorial waters of India extend into the sea to a distance of twelve nautical miles ...ured from the appropriate base line.

1. Location map.

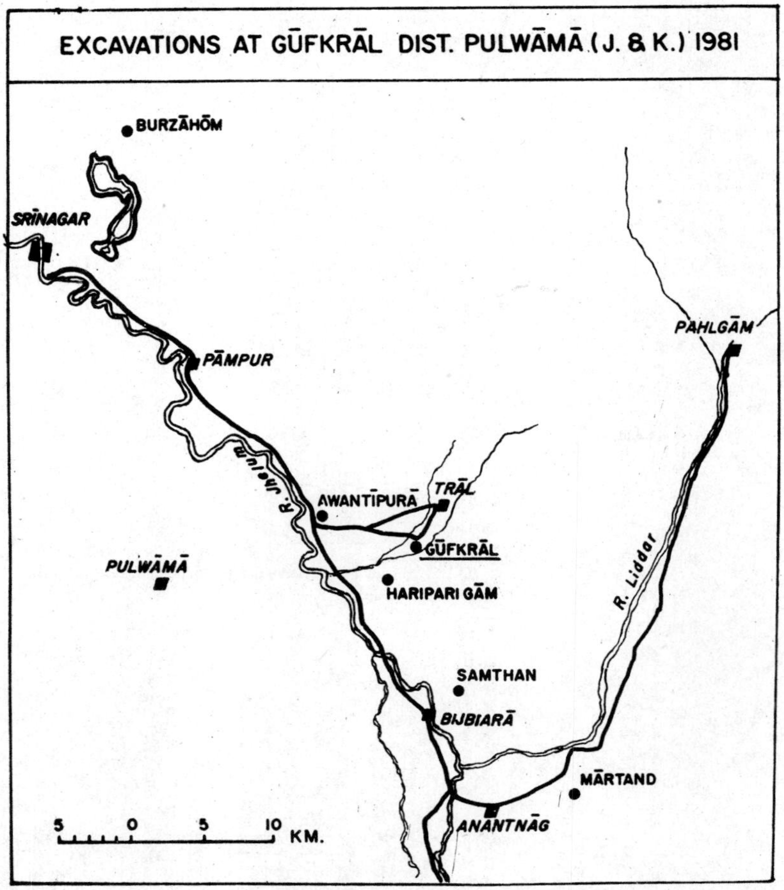

2. Detailed location map.

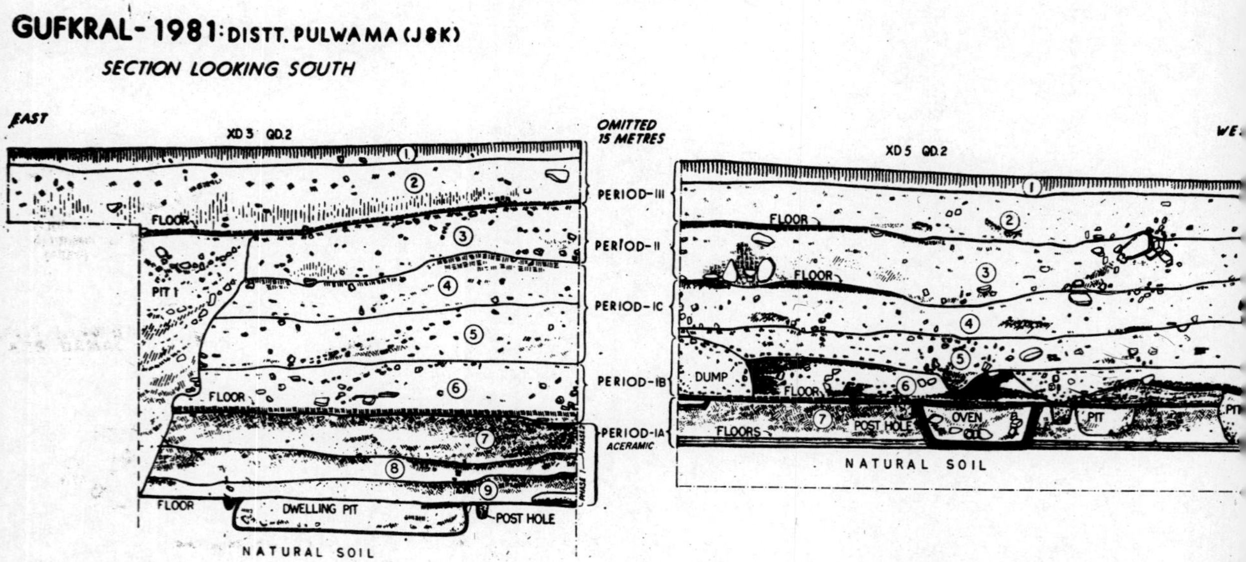

3. Gufkral - Section showing occupational deposits.

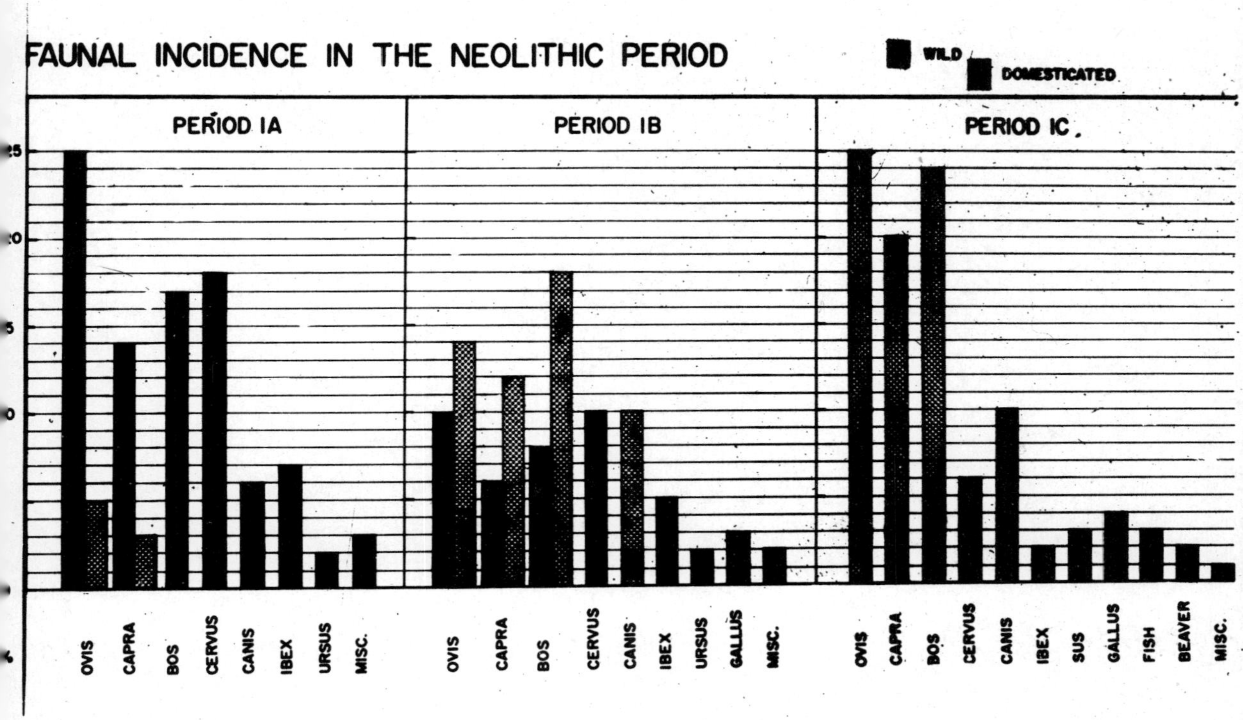

4. Gufkral - Faunal incidence in the Neolithic period.

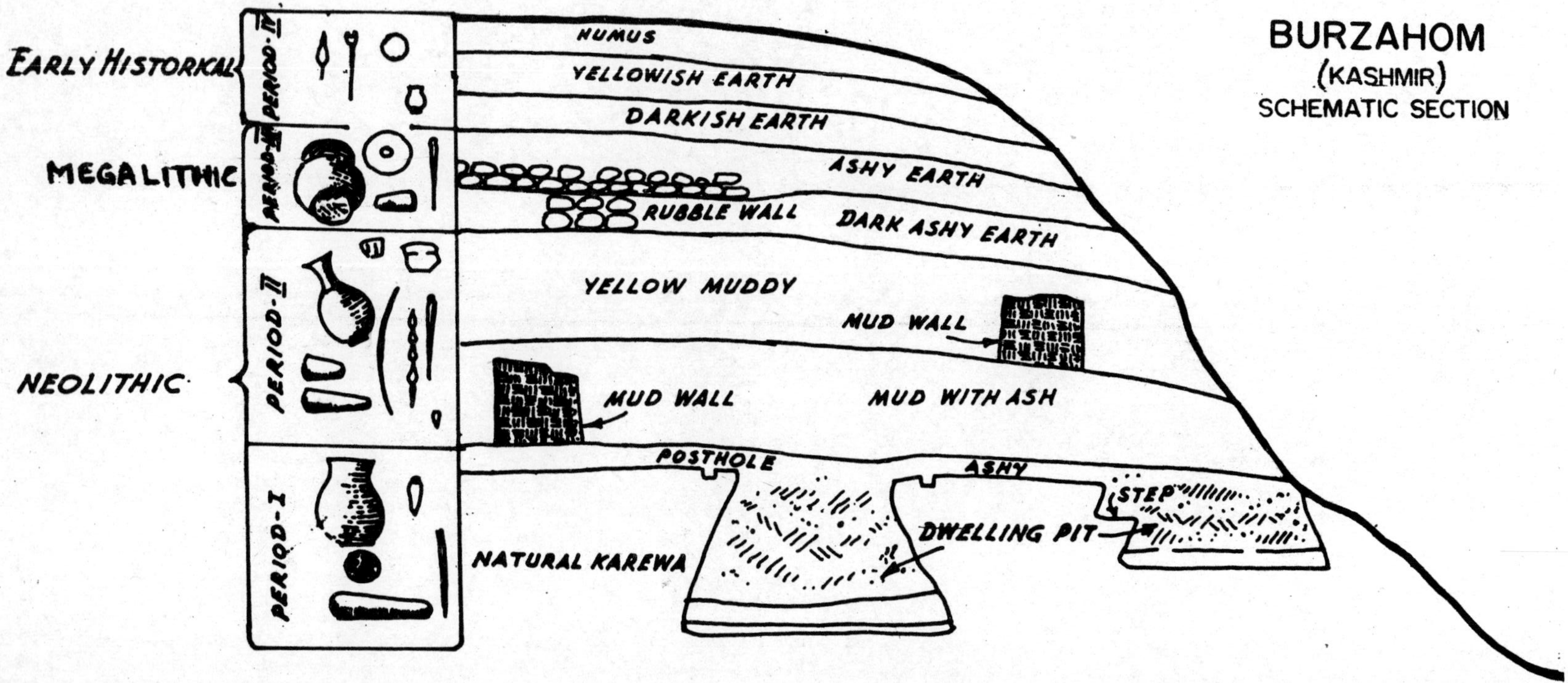

5. Burzahom - Schematic section showing occupational periods.

I. Geological section showing fossil records.

II. Karewas: Section showing lower and upper karewa deposits and a tectonic fault.

III. Burzahom : General view.

IV. Gufkral : General view showing excavated trenches.

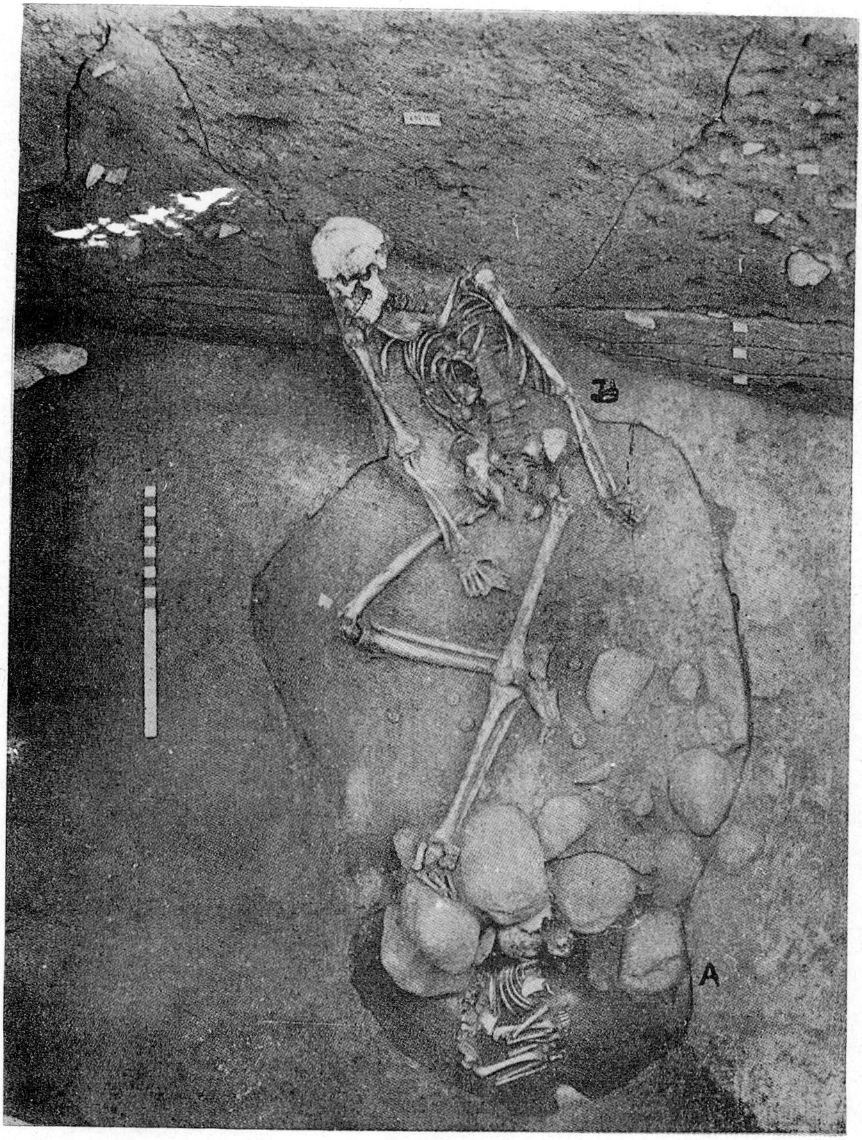

V. Skeleteon No. 1 (adult) and No. 2 (child) of Megalithic and Neolithic period respectively.

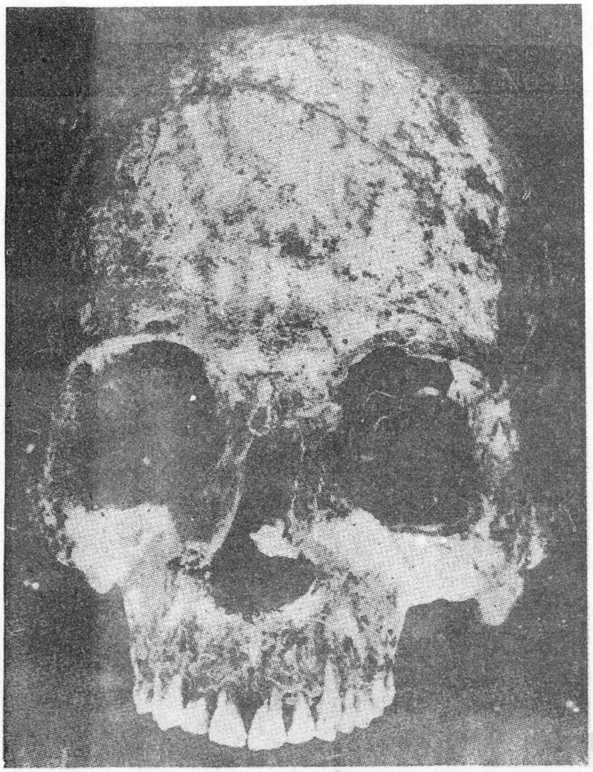

VI. A.Skeleton No.1: Skull-Frontal vie

VI. B. Skeleton No.1: Skull - Laleral view.

VII. Skeleton No. 5.

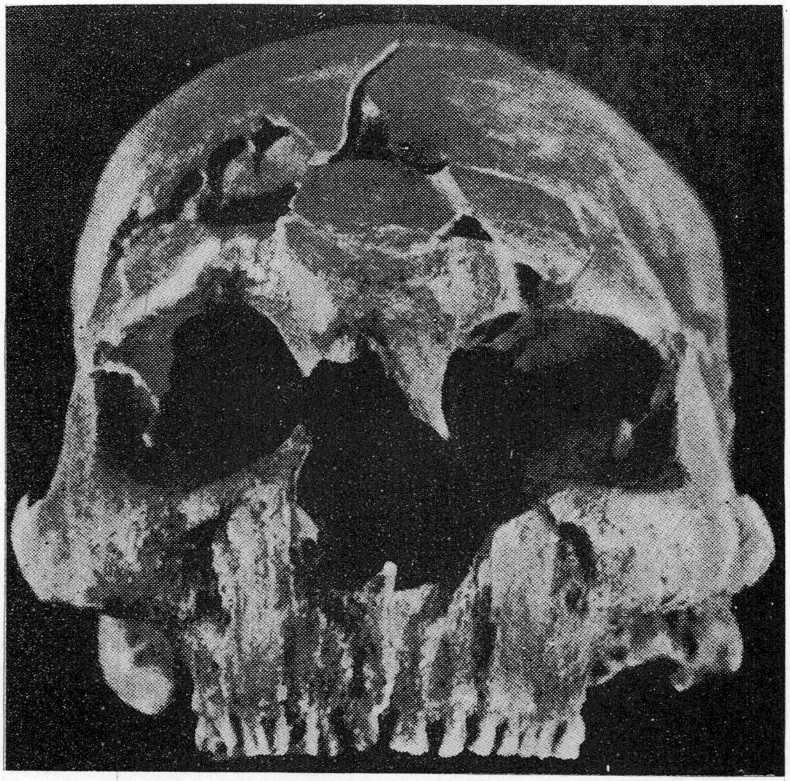

VIII A. Skeleton No. 6: Skull - Frantal view.

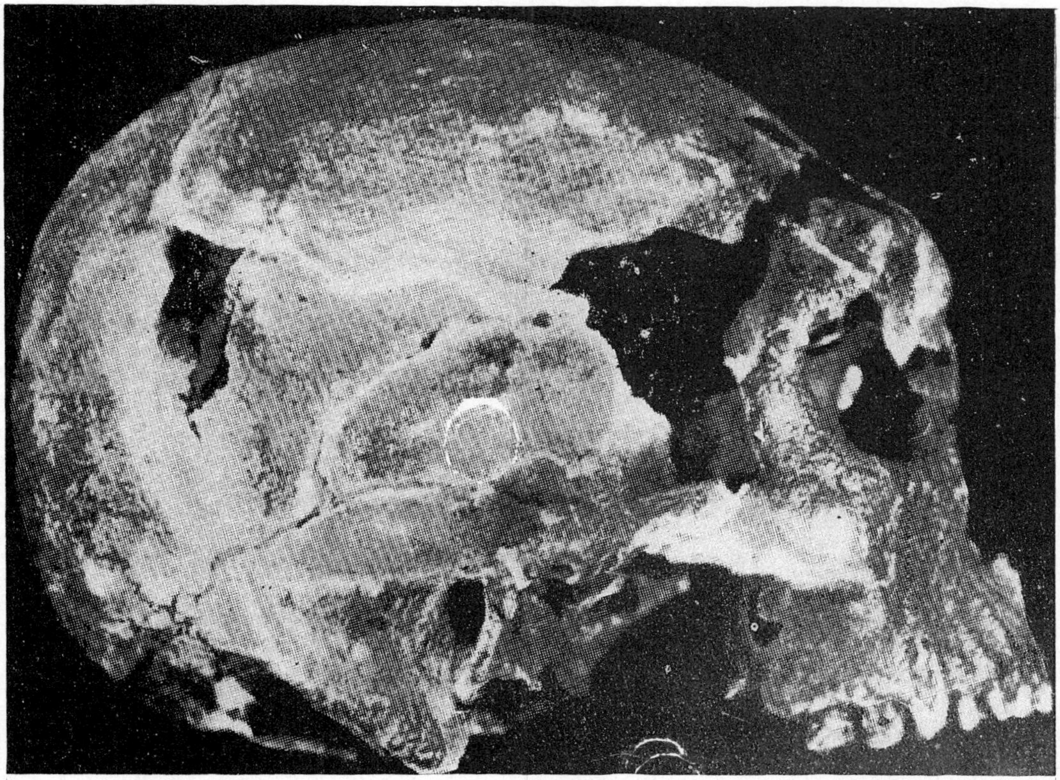

VIII B. Skeleton No. 6: Skull - Right lateral view.

IX. Skeleton No. 7.

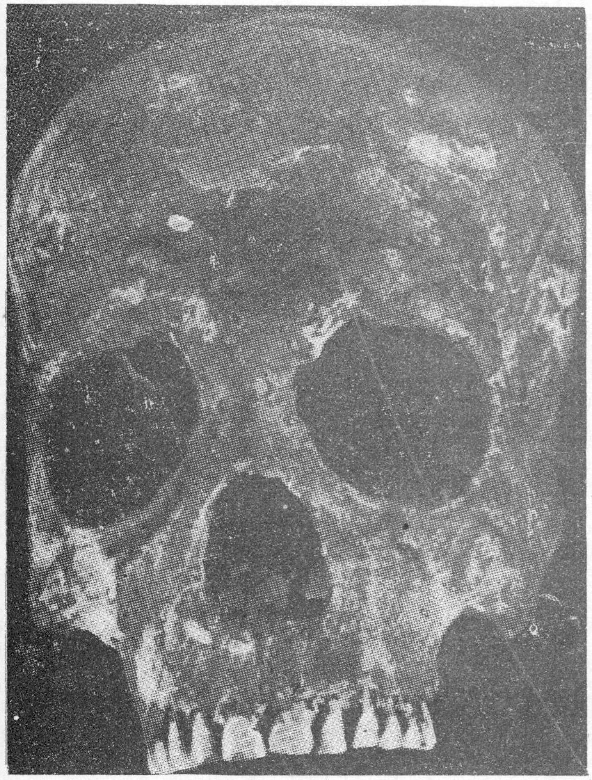

X A. Skeleton No. 7: Skull - frontal view.

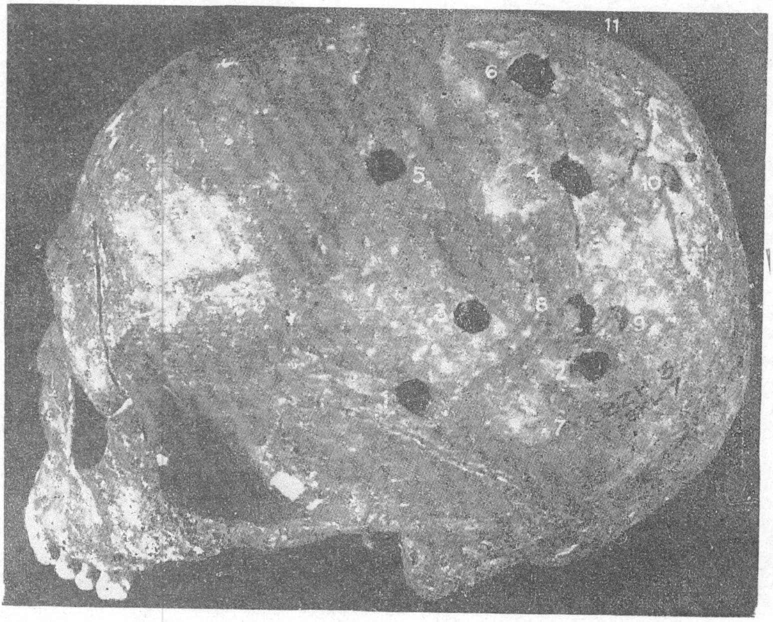

X B. Skeleton No. 7: Skull - Left lateral view showing trephination.

XI. Skeleton No. 8: Neolithic Period II.

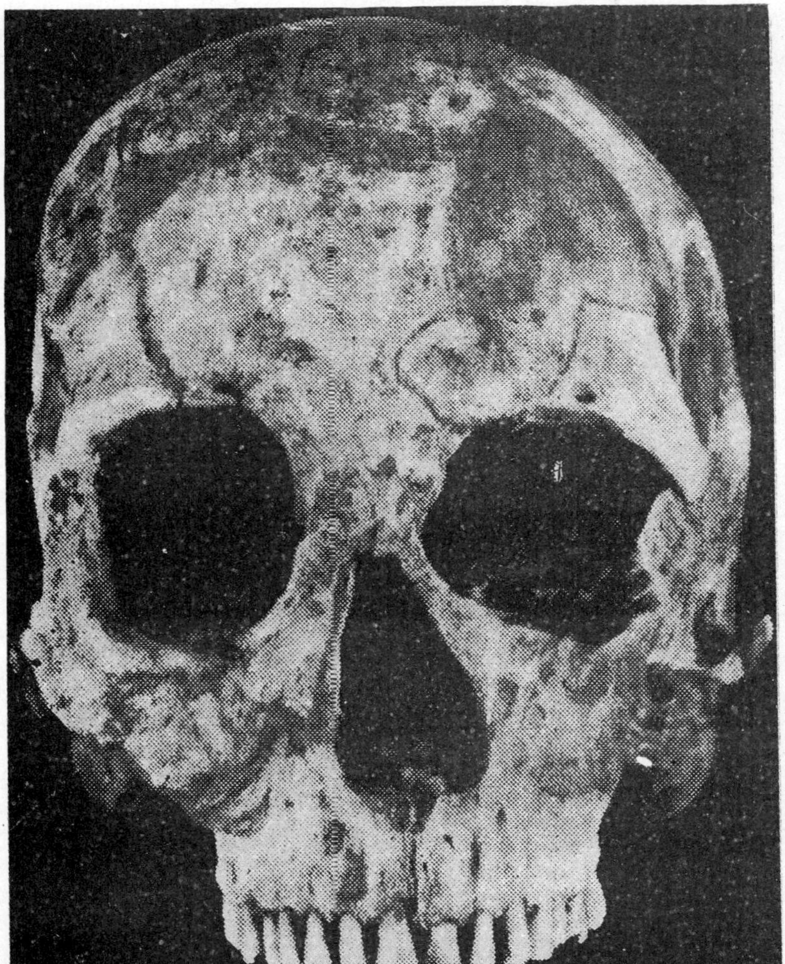

XII. A. Skeleton No 8: Skull - Frantal view.

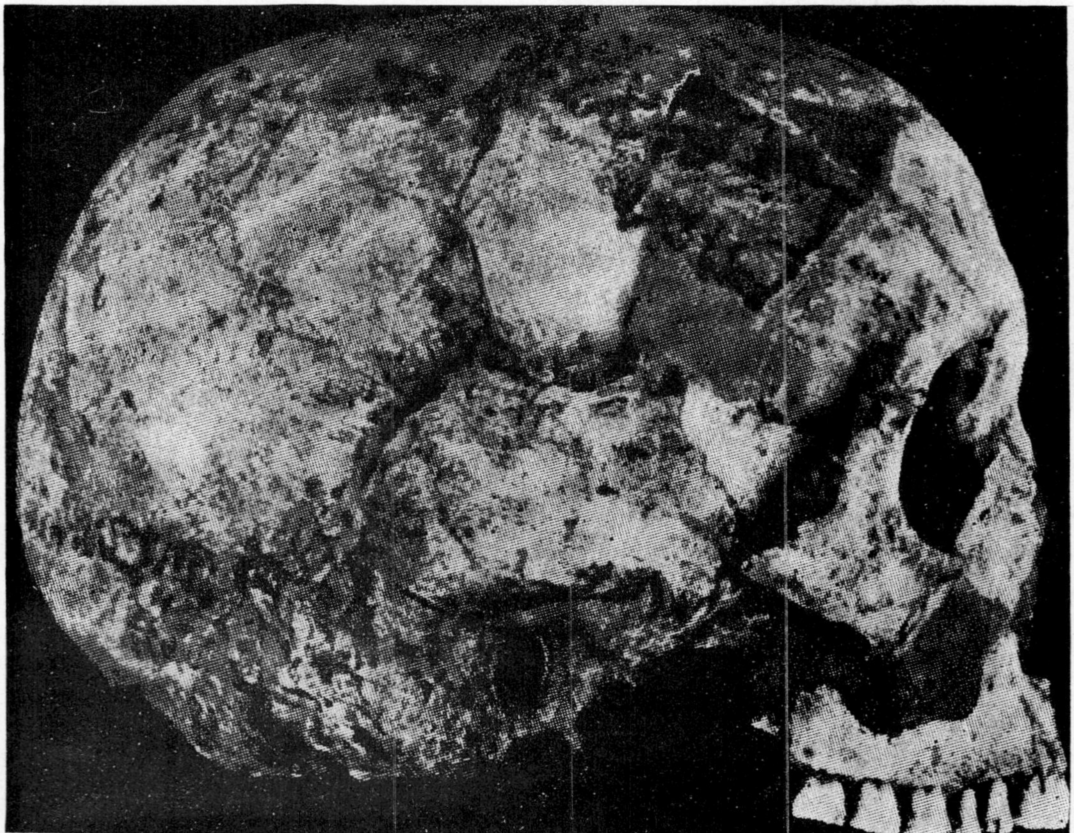

XII. B. Skeleton No. 8: Skull - Right lateral view.

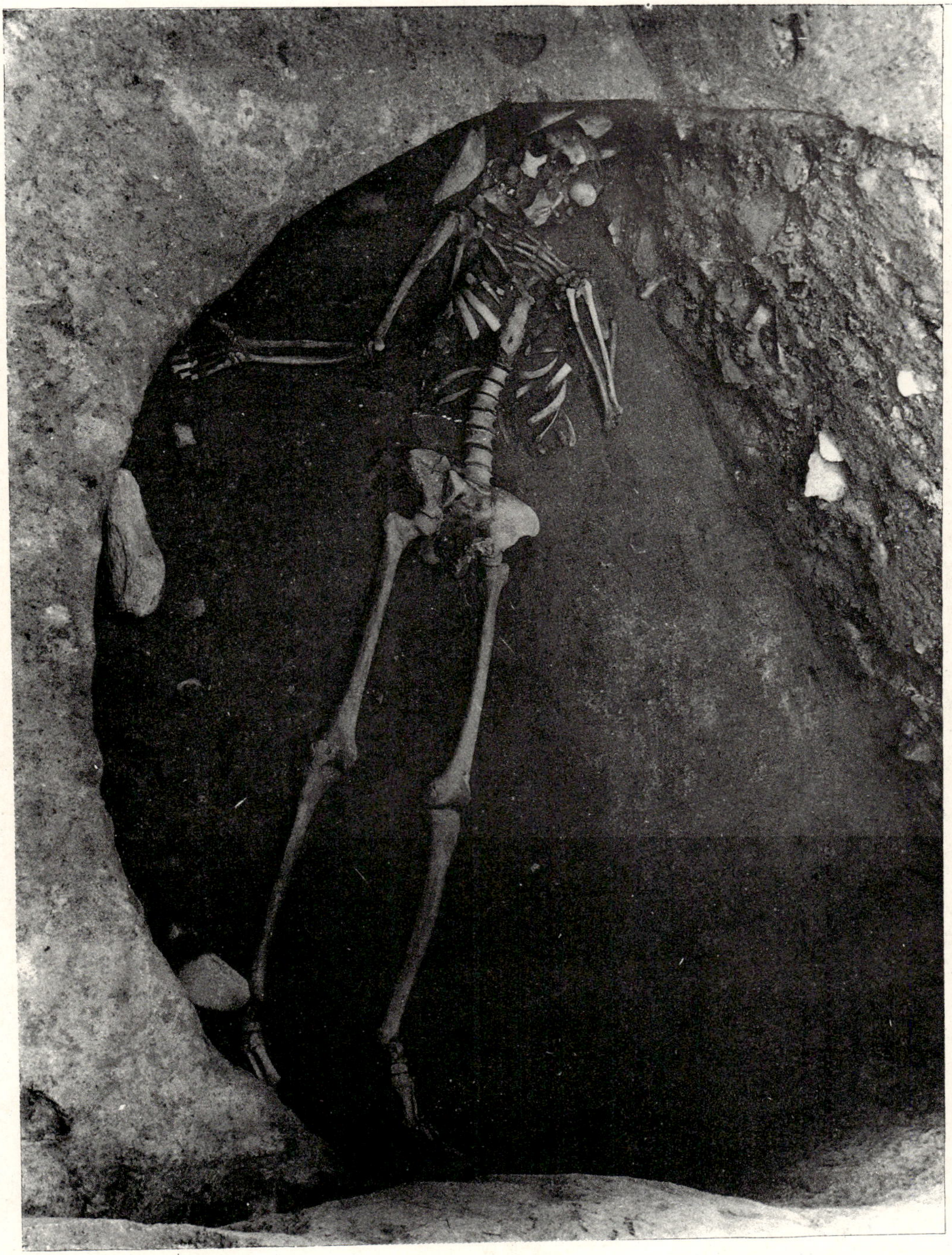

XIII. Skeleton No. 9: Extended burial.

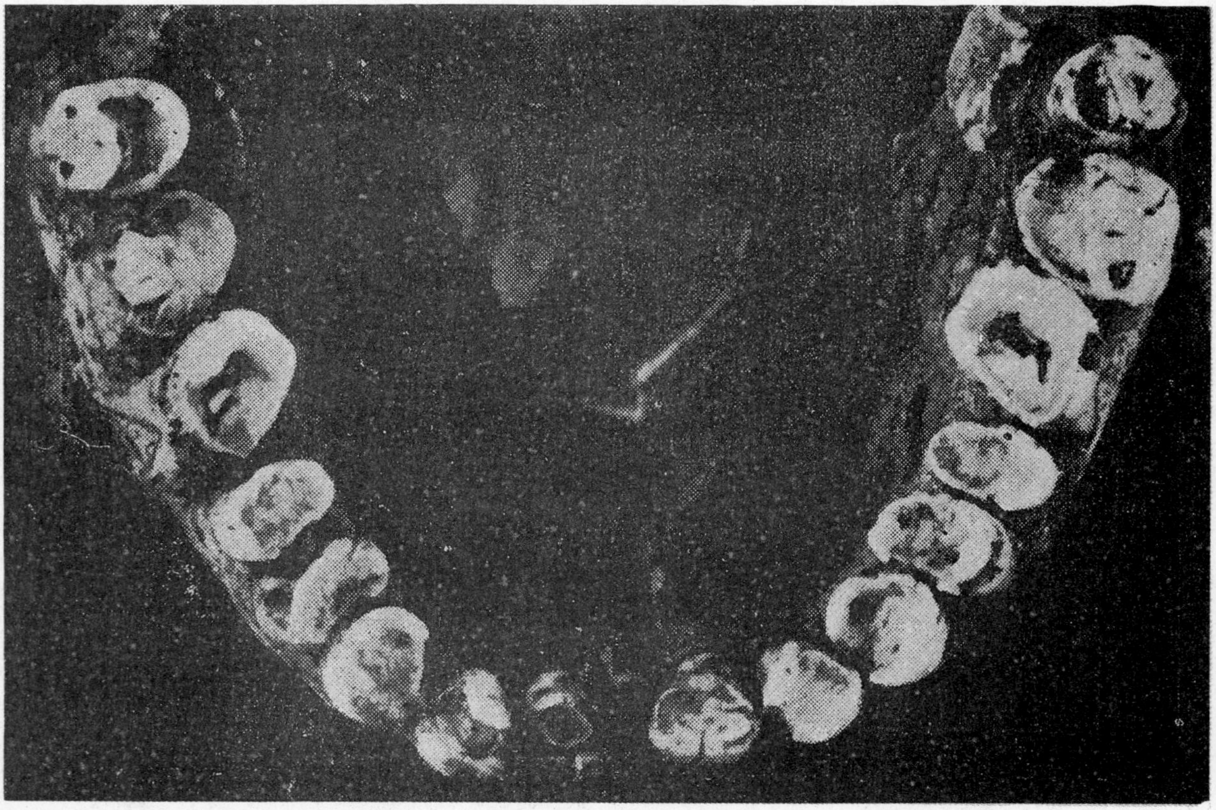

XIV. A. Skeleton No. 6: Mandible teeth showing pulp exposure.

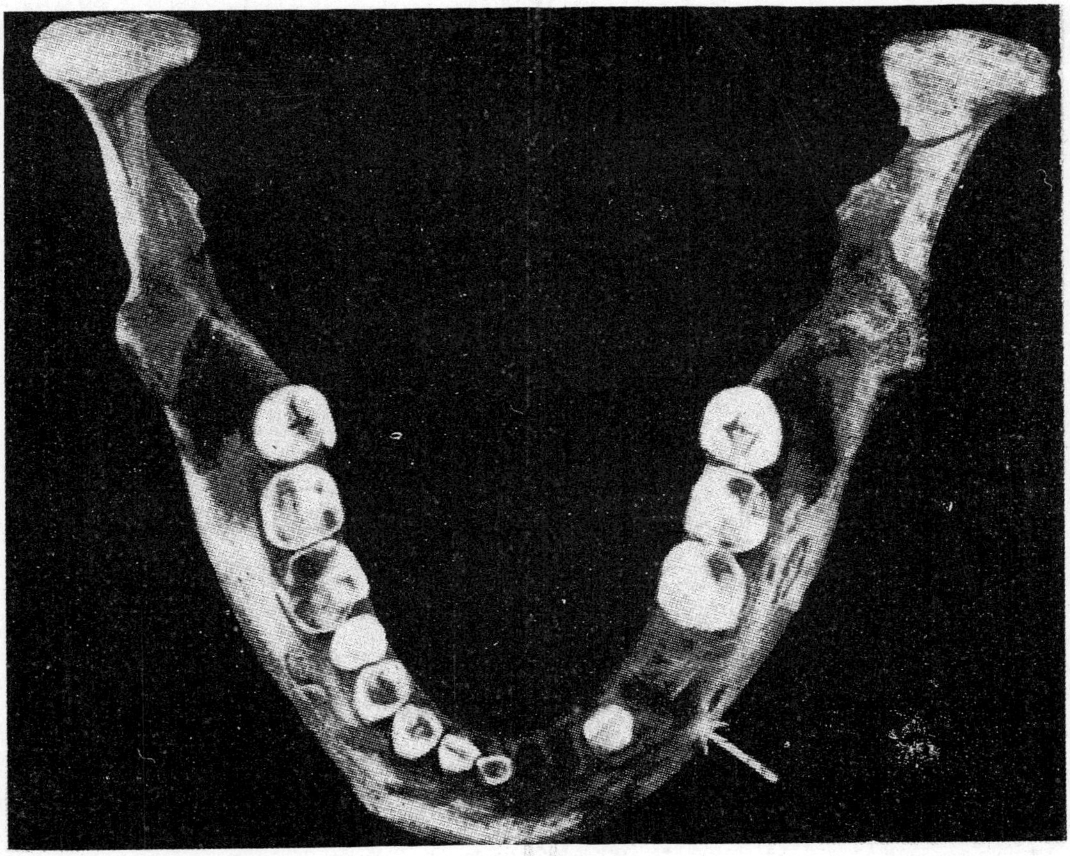

XIV. B. Skeleton No. 8: Mandible teeth showing dental abscess cavity.

XV. Fractional bu[illegible] of wild dogs from period II

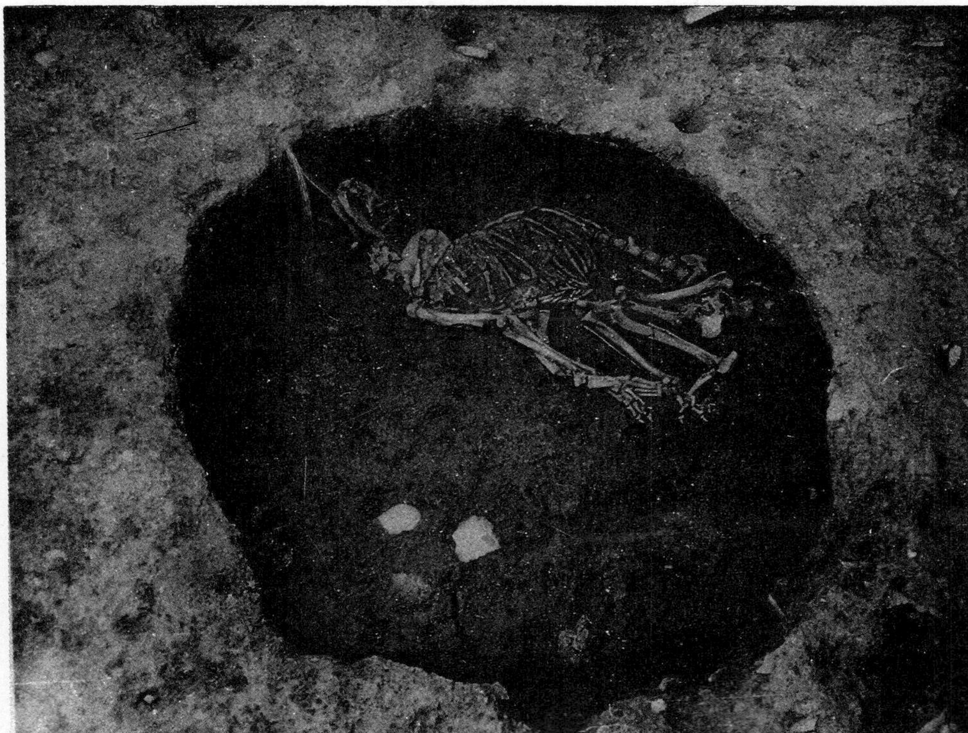

XVIII. Burial of a wolf.

XIX. Burzahom - Hunting scene, Neolithic Period.

XX. Gufkral - Animal Bones - Period IB, Neolithic.

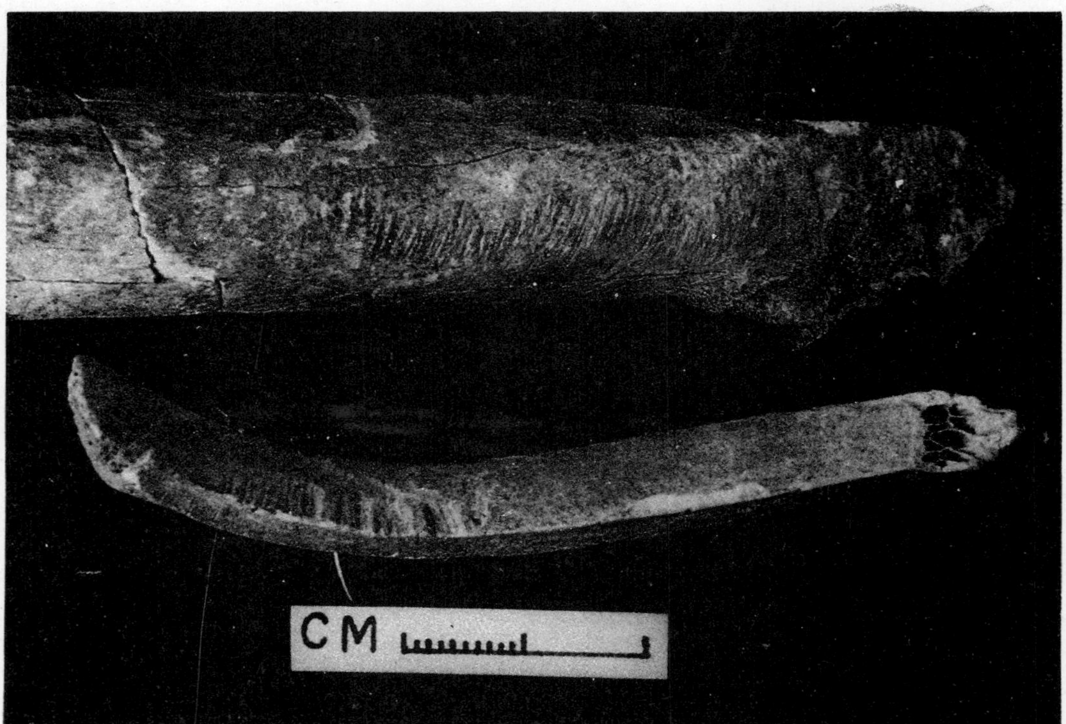

XXI. A. Gulfkral - Scoring marks due to gnawing by the scavanging animal.

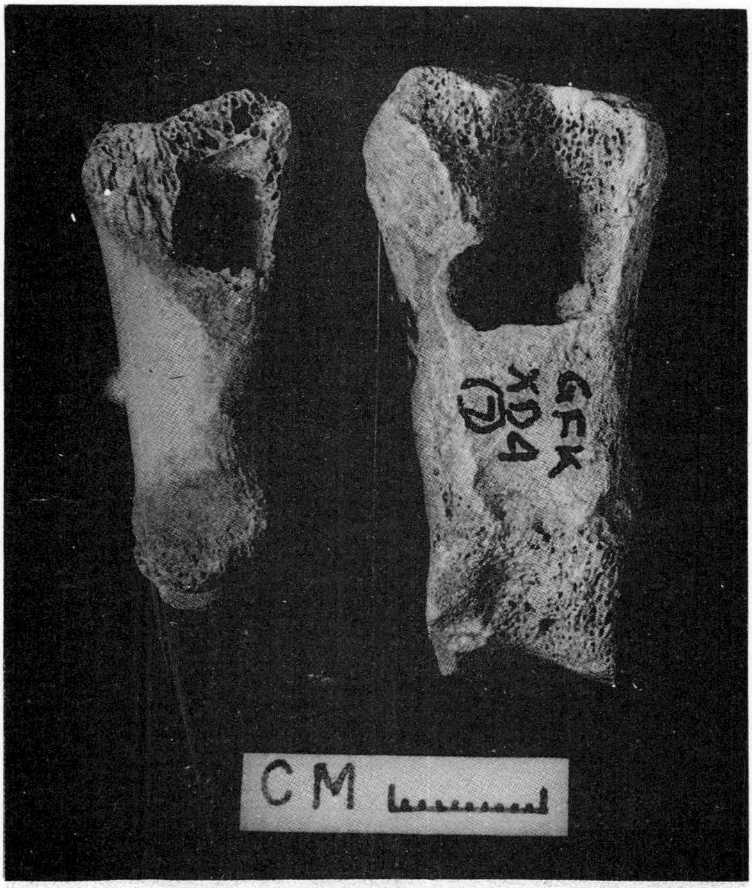

XXI. B. Gulfkral - Holes created in the phalanges for extraction of bone marrow.

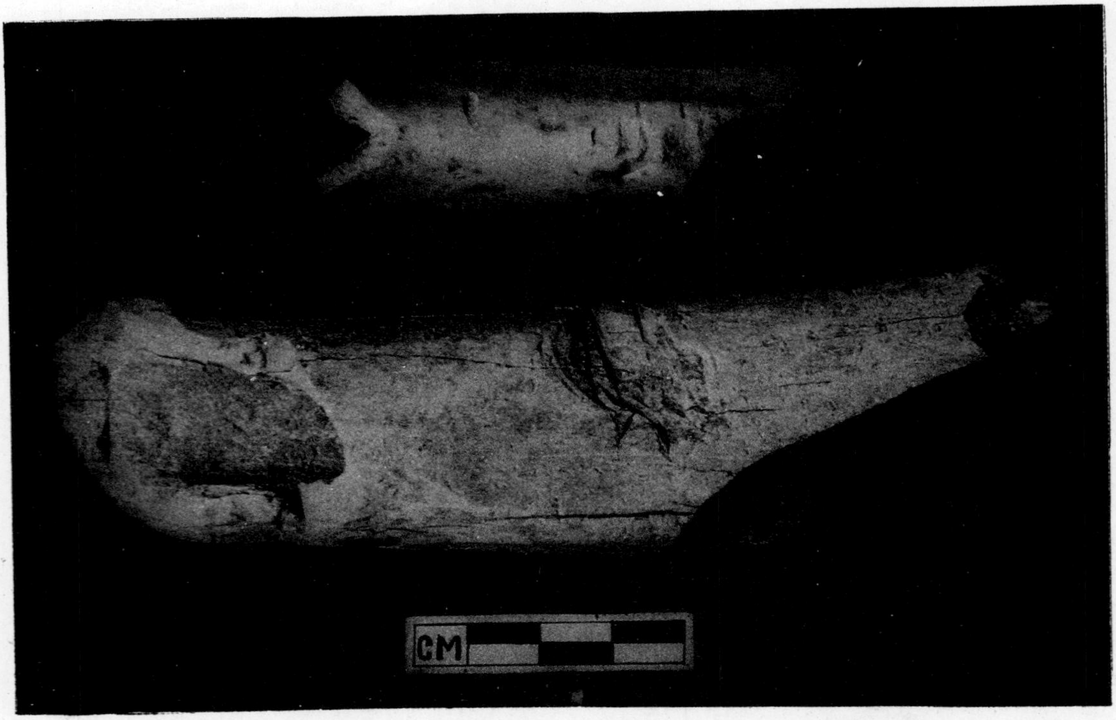

XXII. A. Gulfkral - Filleting and skinning marks.

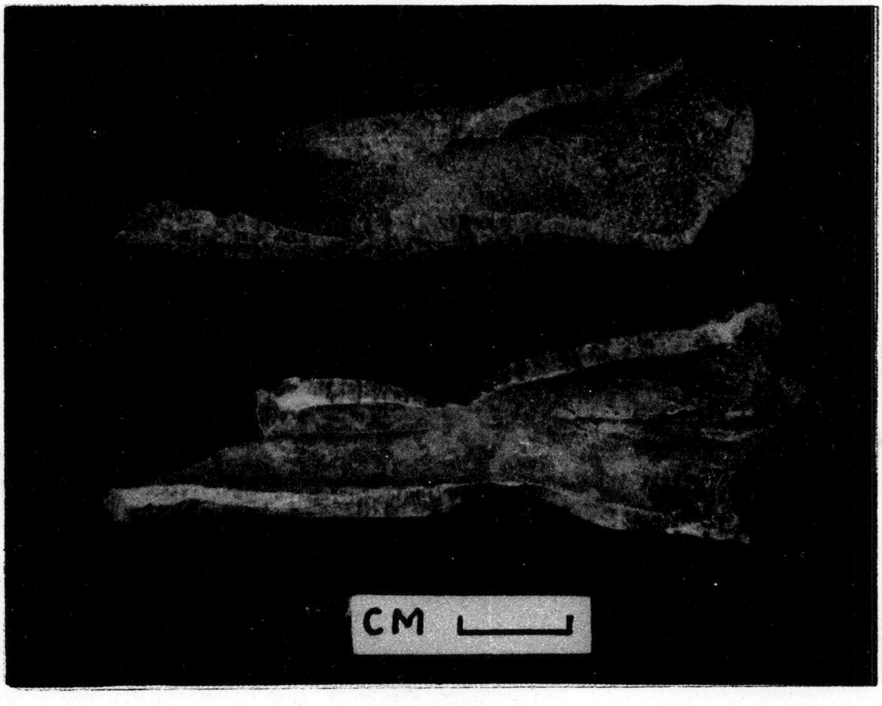

XXII. B. Gulfkral - Teeth marks of the scavanging animal.

XXIII. Gulfkral - Bone Tools - Period IA, Aceramic, Neolithic.